World Stage Press
Verse from the Village

TAKING OFF MY BLACK & WHITE SADDLE SHOES

CLEVELAND POEMS

TAKING OFF MY BLACK & WHITE SADDLE SHOES
CLEVELAND POEMS

MARLANA-PATRICE PUGH HAMER

World Stage Press
Verse from the Village

Taking Off My Black & White Saddle Shoes
Cleveland Poems
© 2024 Marlana-Patrice Pugh Hamer
ISBN: 978-1-952952-65-4

First Edition, 2024

All rights reserved. No part of this publication may be reproduced, distributed, or transmitted in any form or by any means, including photocopying, recording, or other electronic or mechanical methods, without the prior written permission of the publisher, except in the case of brief quotations embodied in critical reviews and certain other noncommercial uses permitted by copyright law.

Printed in the United States of America

Edited by Taylor Fitch
Cover Design by Angelica Cannon & Emily Anne Evans
Layout Design by Travis Entrekin & Emily Anne Evans

For Louvenia Elizabeth Gillispie Pugh, my dearest mom, my first teacher. You always dreamed about publishing your own books. Considering all you gave us, especially your love of words, this poetry book is as much yours as it is mine.

**Love you always,
Marti (Louvenia Jr.)**

Table of Contents

xvii   PREFACE

BABY SHOES

- 5   Walking Down Euclid
- 7   SMILE
- 10   Homage to Big Heads
- 11   Soap and Water
- 12   Daddy Said
- 14   Tony the Great!
- 17   The Balloon in Our Attic
- 18   Tomboy
- 20   Little Sister/Big Sister
- 23   Hooky
- 24   Goodbye, Snuffles
- 26   Jif Peanut Butter

SNEAKERS

- 31   2274 E. 74th Street
- 33   Mom's Hands
- 35   Sugar Cane and Green Beans
- 36   Haibun for Our Mothers' Gardens
- 37   Ready
- 38   Dribble
- 39   Fighting Back Four
- 42   Mr. A. Leonard Jasper
- 43   Milk Chute Queen
- 45   Big Dreams
- 46   Miss Hansen

48	Call Mrs. Frances Mason Franklin
49	Finding Our Tar Beaches
50	Christmas Wrapping Paper and Bows
52	Joy to Our World
53	AmeriVision

BLACK & WHITE SADDLE SHOES

59	The Ballad of Annie: Just Another Media Event
61	Coretta
62	Sacristan
64	Blonde
66	My Black & White Saddle Shoes
68	White Cotillion Dresses
70	Jeez Louise!
72	That Adrian Dominican Nun
74	Big Daddy
76	My First Sea of Misogyny
78	Promgate
81	Possessions
82	The Protest That Never Happened
84	Haiban for Mr. Cotter, Blessed English Teacher
85	Ray Midnight
87	My Michael
89	Black Sage at the Pulpit

HIGH HEELS

93	Shelving Our Library Books
94	CFMP Part I
96	CFMP Part II
97	Your Two-Toned Shoes

98	Do the Hustle!
100	Reefer Madness
102	Pay Day
104	The Pugh Musketeers
106	No French Kisses
109	Short Kings
111	Short Shorts
113	Cleveland Metroparks Love
114	B-I-T-C-H
116	Grad School Blues
118	Here Comes the Bride!
120	Flowers
121	Tethered
122	Our Giant Steps
123	Two-Paycheck Plan
125	High Heels

FLAT SHOES

129	Teacher Assault Boot Camp Training
132	School Fashion Police
134	Teenage Suicide Poem
135	Cleveland on Fire
136	HAVE YOU SEEN HER?
139	BULLY
140	Bus 39 in America
141	Spring Cleaning
143	Chagrin Boulevard
144	Murray Hill
146	Goin' Fishin'
148	Red

150 Dad's Fourth Quarter Pass
151 Apartment Living
154 One LAST DROP of BLOOD

BARE FEET

159 Tower City Kiss
160 Shush!
162 Different Drums, Different Songs
164 Grendels, My Modern Epic Poem
170 Watermelon
172 Sullivan's Island: July 2003
174 This Is a Man's World
176 My Concrete Heart
177 Tasting Rainbows
178 Nina Simone, High Priestess of Our Souls
180 Dear Thomas Jefferson
182 My Babies
184 Remembering Cleveland Snow
186 Talford Family Home Epitaph
187 Flight Lessons
189 Erasure Poem: The Black National Anthem
190 Why Do We Still Sing Those Songs?
192 My Superbad Head of Hair
193 Please Don't Call Me "Marla"
196 Ode to My Glorious Two Feet

199 ACKNOWLEDGMENTS

"I shall become, I shall become a collector of me.
And put meat on my soul."

—Sonia Sanchez

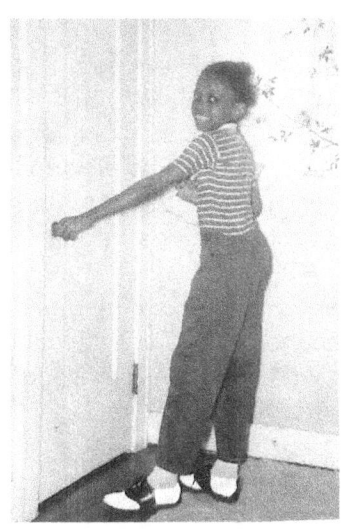

PREFACE

"Our feet tell our stories. They carry us through this life, moving us from one sorrow and season to the next. Our gait can reveal us to be buoyant or bullish, dispirited or steadfast."

—Cicely Tyson, *Just As I Am: A Memoir*

My debut book of poetry was born from my roots, my hometown of Cleveland, Ohio. This entire book is a map of sorts, a tangible representation of where I have walked most of my life. The different shoes I wore. The different paths I took. The different crossroads I encountered. Moreover, this book explains why I must write, why being a poet is such lifeblood for me and many others who are brave enough to keep walking.

Framed in six distinct sections, my poems are about my Cleveland, externally and internally. Some I have performed at open mics and other events. My poems continue to be well-received in artistic settings, and I am very thrilled to share my Cleveland poems with you, dear reader.

This poetry collection focuses on my intersectionality — primarily, what it is like to be both a Woman and Black. In short, many of my poems embody a Black Feminist perspective. Thus, some of my poems are also about misogynoir.

I am a Baby Boomer, significantly influenced by the times and societal norms during my formative years. To give you some perspective, our first television set was a black and white, a box on legs with rabbit ears. There was a large, metal antenna on the roof to pick up the signals. Back then, having a television was like buying the latest iPhone — we all marveled at it every time we watched programs together.

Many significant events and people have made an indelible mark on who I am today. Family, religion, heritage, and education have all impacted my life. Of course, my losses while living in Cleveland have also made me who I am today — stronger and more grateful.

Another important revelation is that my family always considered me the family "librarian"... in other words, our family's archivist. For many years, I have been chronicling our story, keeping track of family history by maintaining old photos and papers. Also doing research. With many loved ones gone, I value this role even more now. In short, this book is as much about my family as it is about me. I owe them a deep debt of gratitude for assigning me this lofty role so early in life. I wear it with pride and look forward to delving more deeply into our roots.

As a work in progress, I continue to be challenged, but I remain steadfast and hopeful. Desiring to fit in, I admit I sometimes still feel assimilation's tug. Even in my formative years, I recognized that many of us are asked to live between at least two worlds. Learning how to navigate code switching, wearing a variety of shoes, can be daunting. Downright confusing. Sometimes disturbing. Even demeaning. For so many of us, deep in our hearts, we simply want to be granted the freedom to feel safe exploring who we are and, then, to be accepted as our authentic selves.

Hopefully, this book of poetry will help many keep living and loving, no matter what differences impede us. Learning how to survive and finding our joy are always essential goals, even when we are oppressed and undervalued. Poems that help heal us are a great starting point, for me and many others. I hope you enjoy walking in my shoes down Euclid Avenue. Then keep stepping on to discover the many important people and places that have shaped me and my world.

Thank you, reader.

TAKING OFF MY BLACK & WHITE SADDLE SHOES

CLEVELAND POEMS

BABY SHOES

"Moms, take it from me; do not buy your baby too many shoes when they're so tiny, because their feet grow every week."

—Ciara

Walking Down Euclid

Born in December, muddy snow and bristling air soon became family. Walking down Euclid Avenue, Cleveland's heartbeat street, in arms or inside a stroller, my eyes did all my walking.

When I upgraded to holding Mom's hand, my little feet, eager to go into all the shoe stores lining the street not paved in gold. Felt like it was. Many places, we took all day deciding on Easter clothes. Went to Woolworth's for chili or the May Company to buy Frosties. Candy and nuts were in the basement. Beloved hot dogs at Kresge's.

Got blue, patent-leather shoes from Sears on Carnegie. Bought white fishnets at one Euclid store. Blue-and-white floral suit so cute. Always ahead of trends again. None of us ever dressed like everybody else back then. Even the laughter never stopped us.

Those little shops. Forgot all the names. Never the big ones — Higbee's, May Company, Halle's. Rich people, always associated with the latter. White women in their minks going to lunch in the restaurant on upper floors for uppity people. I think they actually had two. The other not exactly for us either. Not until it was almost closed for good. Now an office building.

Which reminds me of the Christmas window displays. Always came downtown to see Higbee's. All the moving parts of Santa and his helpers. And the music. *"Mr. Jingeling. How you tingaling? Keeper of the keys."* Used to be at Halle's for the holidays. Also on TV, Channel 5. I think we saw him in person once. He was never a young man. No Black Santas yet.

I was never on Euclid for any of the parades, except St. Paddy's which is nothing like New York's or Chicago's. No disrespect. Our Euclid showpiece, Cleveland Orchestra's 4th of July concerts on the Square. My favorite reason to be on Euclid. Hop on Shaker Rapid Blue. 15 Minutes to Tower City.

Used to work off Euclid at CSU's library. Lunchtime shopping and people-watching, catching the loop a daily hoot. Took classes at Cleveland State in later years. A little night music for that experience makes me want to sing.

Even when Euclid became more blighted and scary, took Waldenbooks and the Old Arcade away, still found reasons to walk there. Sit for a while. Stay. Celebrated my parent's 50th at the Renaissance. Ate at Sans Souci. French food, not soul food. Mom and Dad loved the ambience. She got to sing with the pianist. Hotel probably has another name by now. Wasn't it once Stouffer's?

Met with my Black lawyer in his ritzy suite in the Hanna Building. Street food sold nearby, you could sit outside and eat in the theater district with Wi-fi, digital ticker tape showing at least someone's still thriving. But more and more businesses not surviving.

Years later, "Crazy walking there late at night!" When the streetlights were my only companions, could still sleepwalk it on a dare. If the lottery was attached to how many paces I took on Euclid Avenue, would be a billionaire.

SMILE

Mom always said I came out of her womb smiling.
Dimples ready to twinkle on cue
that snowy, magnificent morning.
The day after Christmas.
Or was it just gas? *Not a genuine smile*.
I believe it *was* a smile.
Newborns, they say, only have early "reflex smiles."
The real ones *technically* don't appear until six to twelve weeks after birth.
Gradually, my smile became an emblem.
Even when my brain and other insides weren't yet suited up for life's complexities,
I became known for my
SMILE!

Some like to say people who smile on call are phonies.
Check. I have been called *phony*
by some friends, some relatives.
Some say it outright.
The polite, the tacit.
Innuendos and implications.
Even smirks.
A coworker once said, "Oh, you're that teacher that smiles a lot!"
His derisive tone was a backhanded compliment
lying there like a truculent, but malnourished dog.

Yes, conditioning is part of our American-made DNA, so
all of us know when and where we should be smiling.
Selfies.
Graduations. Weddings. Classes.
Selfies.
Zoom Meetings. Job Interviews. Family Dinners.
Selfies.
Baby Showers. Retirement Parties.
Selfies.
You get the idea.

Honesty: We've all had to wear fake smiles
on at least one traditionally *happy* occasion.

More conditioning.
I watched *Howdy Doody* as a child.
Doofus puppet always smiling!
So was that annoying Kool-Aid pitcher.
Please do not tell me I have a Kool-Aid smile!
Another backhanded compliment. Well, I do have nice white teeth.
Some are right to say we have lots of reasons
to never
smile.
In a straw poll, I bet most of us would say
we see more full-out grimaces daily
than pleasant smiles painted on our faces.
Every day, I catch myself smiling, especially when I look into my mirror.
Not because I am conceited,
But — with a Gigantic B —
because my smile is genuinely
Me!
A way I celebrate living.
No need to check for my authenticity.
Like a tat on your arm, it's just *Me* being *Me!*

If you continue to label me otherwise,
you deserve another booby prize.
I love smiling.
I love laughing.
Period!
To be very clear — never to hurt or harm anyone.
Even when I truly hurt enough to cry,
I will find a way back to my SMILE and giggles.
Even after arguments, breakups, surgeries, funerals, debts, damn taxes.
Countless inequities.

Smile, though your heart is aching. Smile, even though it's breaking.
Like the song says,
Just SMILE!
Happy chemicals hit your brain like Hampton University's marching band performing on another field at halftime.
Dopamine, Serotonin, and Endorphins putting on a glorious show.
That Drum Major E, always spectacular!
All because of real (or fake)
SMILES on faces —

Bonus prize —
others may also start to feel better.
Let's keep that smile loop going —
also for Laughter.

Problem is, so many of us are still wearing masks these days.
Solution? SMILE with your eyes —
even your body!
It worked for Charlie Chaplin. Didn't it?

Homage to Big Heads

Bread box. Pumpkin.
Kids called us WATERHEADS.
People saw me as a baby
coming, sitting, standing in a crowd.
Loved *Mr. and Mrs. Potato Head*.
They could speak without moving their mouths.

People inquired, "Why that size?"
Proud Mama and Daddy gave me life.
My cranium grew and grew cause it's
inflated with knowledge.
If it wasn't this big, I would not
have done so well in college.
Wore the biggest mortarboard
they had in stock.

My mushroom cloud head soon found out
there's plenty outside our block.
Not always the bigger, the better.
Big or small outside,
what's inside always matters.

Soap and Water

Fancy liquids, creamy or foamy —
promises of eternal beauty, thinness,
wrinkle removal. Milder enjoyments
for mothers, daughters, and sisters now.
Water, sometimes tepid,
sometimes like cleats walking across sensitive skin.
Not much to lather about, searching for compliments.

When I was little, Mom washed my face
with Ivory soap and water in the morning,
stinging my eyes,
rinsing off residue.
Cold water tightening pores.
Dabbing me with a tiny washcloth
that smiled with us under the light.
It had dimples like me.

Mom always smiled, said I was pretty.
Two sisters peeking into the bathroom,
waiting their turn.
We made so much lather,
enough to make anyone feel lovely!
Soap-and-water lessons in bathrooms
when we're young.
Hands ready to cradle mother's wisdom.

Daddy Said

He said quietly, *Don't look!*
We were standing in line at an inner-city store.
Just my Dad and me in a place
where you buy what you need,
then leave
as quickly as you came.
Not a place like home with curtains,
friendly ceilings.
I dutifully complied.
His little soldier girl
never asked him what he meant.

Haunts me I never did.
My guess?
Dad had become my overcoat again.
Didn't want anyone to see
my inquisitive eyes looking
straight at them, deciphering people,
puzzle pieces that just do not fit.
Kids do that when
thrust into adult worlds.
I would rather have been playing.

Grown up, I don't always look
straight into eyes. Sometimes sideways.
Not even relatives. Only those I trust.
Long ago, Black folks weren't allowed
to lock onto certain eyes.
Daddy probably told me that early.

Eyes looking. Forced into others' sins
on platters at dinner tables.
Serving food you don't want or need.
Meat hooked up in back rooms,
flies circling all around.
Men shoot you for knowing,
even back then.
Just like they do now.

When I was just a little kid
forced to see life
before I was ready.

Dad and Mom always called the shots,
with Dad as admiral,
keeping me and my siblings as
kids, looking into harmless drawers
for probably too long.
Innocence always a keepsake.

Tony the Great!

Sometimes, my father would spontaneously say,
I am Tony the Great!
Before. Then, after his weekend jaunts.
Alone. He had to go alone.
Part ego and mythbuilder.
A signature affirmation. His coat of arms.
A chest thump for himself, like how
Tarzan always had to forage,
yell out in his jungle
without Jane.
An emblem. An escape.
A way to become whole.
Iconic for a wife, children, and adoring subjects.
Never as tall as Cousin Rafer,
yet always taller than any man.

Tony the Great! was once the definition.
A fine man catching gazes on boulevards.
After going to see *Porgy and Bess*,
mistaken for Poitier.
Similar grace and dark skin.
Young Tony
wore a stocking cap at night to create the Ultimate
Slicked-back hair with a perfect mustache.
And *Oh!* those deep-dish dimples,
deeper than his sweet potato pies,
always getting deeper.
Standing in better for Billy Dee,
courting hit movies
or kissing delicate hands after a conquest.

Daddy, the dresser impresser.
Where is that zoot suit picture Mom showed us once?
Telling us how she taught you how to match after that,
standing there in all those stripes with your brother John.
Hat with the exaggerated brim.
Sunglasses, later shields from unwanted stares.

Privacy, a growing coveted accessory, and
older Brother John,
The Talker with the seismic laugh,
your knight.
Both of you wore suits like armor
never slaves to jeans. Nor anything.
Knowing admirers and clothes spilling from closets
never make *Daddies* or *Great Men!*

A different shade and pedigree,
Dad could have been a Chappie James
or a Benjamin O. Davis,
another one of his heroes.
Daddy was more homeboy George Washington Carver
mixed with *griot,* a hip John Hope Franklin.
Telling us about Ham's children.
Hannibal might really be Black.
Sitting in his chair like a lettered scholar born with privileges,
Daddy polished African diamonds and theories daily.

He was the *Man* who governed our physical world.
Complex Man. Rodin's *The Thinker*.
Pragmatic about migrating North
to Cleveland in the 40s.
Stint in the Army.
Thought. Then did.
Gave up GI Bill-tailored dreams for car industries,
A stay-at-home Donna Reed wife he called "Dynamite!"
Also "Mouse," cause she liked cheese —
a nuclear family.
Mongrel named *Ditto*.
Parakeet named Joey broke his neck trying to get out of his cage.
Daddy conquered traffic. His responsibilities. Daily.
Never late for work or anniversaries.
Or a chance to kiss Mom while dancing slow.
Always bringing home bags of fresh foods,
his favorite plunders to share.

Dad, the *Shapeshifter*.
The Thinker with more than more heart.
Made skim milk his Hennessy.
Abandoned cigars stinking up our cars.
Home early on Saturday nights.
Stayed home with us watching
Moonstruck and PBS operas.
AME Church on Sundays, followed by
long brunches, sometimes at Houlihan's.
Kept dancing with Mom.
Going to family concerts and shows,
Sammy Davis Jr., Al Green.
Every summer, repaved his driveway alone.
Raked more and more leaves in the backyard.
Kept shoveling snow until his back said, *NO!*
Then wore a dumb party hat on his 80th birthday.
One of his greatest feats during his reign!

Checked on relatives constantly.
Sent checks when he couldn't.
Cooking family meals while neglecting himself.
Still trying to show us how to sew for ourselves.
Laughing, watching rusty, grown *Us* sleeping

in his prized chair.

The Balloon in Our Attic
for BroWiley, aka Tim

Baby brother, three years my junior, a shadow that followed me everywhere until he started noticing his own. He could walk then, so his stubby legs were his fascination, leading him up forbidden stairs to that window of all windows, open on the landing. Looking down, all solid driveway below that would take him (or anyone) home.

Guess Mom left it open cause there was no air conditioning. Just screens you could pop out when sweat decided to play games with our eyebrows. Our foreheads. Our smelly armpits. "Do not go in the attic without permission. Without Dad, Mom, or older sisters!" She always said, sounding like herself. "Never play up there!"

Must have been hot that day. Baby bro's brain working hard to find cool spaces to expand. I found him at that open window of windows. He was gasping for air with one of his tiny fingers reaching beyond cobwebs for places little kids should never go.

Loving him more than my own life. My emphatic arms grasping tightly around his waist. Screaming with every part of me, louder than Mom ever allowed. Screaming loud enough for God to hear! I feared our only brother's imaginary balloon tugging to take his tuft of unruliness away from us. Forever! Confused baby bro knew. He let go of that faltering balloon. Let it sail downward without him. I held my dearer than dear brother tighter after that day.

Tomboy

One of the worst days of my life.
Mommy said I could no longer go outside
bare-chested like my little brother.
Up until then, he and I were
two pieces of an Almond Joy.
Equally delicious.

Sometimes equally mischievous,
aggravating the walls and ceilings inside.
Yet this scrawny kid with
barely any hair on his head
now had more rights
than five-going-on-six girls like me.
Giving up bare skin
is a constitutional offense!

Why all the commotion?
The suspenders covered up my nubs.
Then gravity shifted.
I was told my short overalls
had to go unless
I wore a top underneath.
I almost cursed God when my
elbow resters kept getting bigger and
bigger. So, my little overalls
were put away in a drawer
that agonized over the dilemma
almost as much as I struggled
later with crazy contraptions called *Bras!*

I could not bear to wear my overalls
with mandatory coverage.
Missing my freedom,
I soon had to learn to forget.
Enduring enemies of armpits.
Lost sleep turning side to side.
Rising up, I might capsize.
Having breasts harder than homework.
Eventually growing to a D cup. Big enough.

Tomboy? Some do not believe I ever played rough
and tumble with my brother.
Or with other boys, like Moon across the street.
Never any injuries or police reports.
Just kids full of joy.
Playing tag. Hide-and-go-seek.
Dodgeball. Racing our Schwinns
up and down our street,
trying to forget the humidity.   Trying to catch butterflies with bare hands.

Little Sister/Big Sister

Part 1

In my universe, birth order is
random, like shuffling cards
while playing bid whist.
Or having your ticket
picked out of a raffle hat.
I have won when chance was
my only possibility.

But being the little sister,
I had no choice.
Consigned to have the door
closed on my face, almost smacking my nose,
when my sisters had their private football huddles.
Consigned to go play scrimmage with
my little brother because my older sisters
chose to stay inside and ignore me.
I did not know anything,
according to them and their friends,
no longer finding me interesting —
if they ever did.
Funny, because they were never
much older than me.
Not really.

Time came when I realized
my baby brother and I were bulk-ordered.
His package was just delayed.
Sometimes we played house
with our little kids' faux marble table.
Or we drew together.
Me, loving to draw black
borders around his people.
Not sure why.
He never complained.
I hijacked his red wagon to carry around
all my summer-reading books.
Looked pretty cool pulling books behind me outside.

No other kid in the neighborhood ever did.
Pegeen was one of my first books read.
Another summer, I read *The Catcher in the Rye*.
Don't think I had that one in the wagon.
I used to eat my brother's leftovers
off his dinner plate.

Yes, time came when
he went to the playground without me.
But my brother never made me
feel like I was disposable.
That's the difference.
I was his Big Sister. Not Little Sister
who bowed down, shined shoes,
held trains of evening gowns
for her older sisters.

Part 2

If I had been the firstborn,
how different would my life be right now?
Older sisters get there first.
Any mistakes they made,
my parents threw up hazard signs and blockades
for the rest of us.
They were afraid that imitation would mean catastrophe.
They often forgot to let us all freestyle and backstroke for ourselves.

Me, no synchronized swimming trophies.
No chance becoming the next aquatic goddess,
the Black Esther Williams.
At the Fairfax rec center, my middle sister
sank all of that. Panicked, almost drowned.
Could not finish her first lesson,
reinforcing my parents' belief that their children
never needed to learn how to float
or hold their own breath underwater.
Assuming Black folks aren't tadpoles,
even though we came from water.

Part 3

Then Mom and Dad insisted I stay.
Every mention of going away
to college was met with their protest signs. Their barricades.
Mr. Jasper jokingly said my parents wanted to keep us.
Even after friends were delivering their kids
FedEx to the nearest out-of-state university
or HBCU. Howard was our Harvard.
Fisk was our Yale.

Black parents, not ours, were
converting their children's rooms into storage.
My best college offer, Wellesley.
The White version of Spelman.
Highly regarded, even before anyone
ever heard of Hillary Clinton.
I still have the acceptance letter.
One of my favorite trophies.

Hooky

The footlocker waits in the middle of the dining room floor
displaced, like me on the first day of school,
not wanting to release my mother's hand
to sing songs indoors without her
to learn an alphabet I already knew
or nap before painting fakery. Clouds out of sight,
yet I am the clouds, menacing this school's
enclosed *Gray* walls.
Rather play sick and sit gleefully on our porches,
make mud pies. Fall in mud while
Yellows engulf and
Oranges empower me to dumpster dive off swings.
Hips just right for Hula Hoops on half days
or days when I had slight fevers from growing so fast,
always recovering soon enough to finish
my "vacations" in the middle of a lawn, drenched in exhilaration,
dew inspiring more *Greens* than *Browns*.
Me, making sure skates don't crash into all that plastic *Pink* —
Mom's fragile flamingos will protest.
Looking.
Forewarning me, never touch or speak to other truants until much later.
The Central Avenue winos passing by.
Their *Blues* near our gate did not frighten me.
Songs can be searches for tonics or bromides.
I still love to sing and play
outside, looking up at real clouds,
looking down at an oak tree's changing shadows on the ground.
Especially my own, while
celebrating the *Blues*, the *Pinks*. All the real colors.
Brilliant colors
Mom taught me to love.

Goodbye, Snuffles

Goodbye, my stuffed hound dog.
Slightly bigger than my clasped hands.
Brown and tan.
Stiff body built to last — and has.
Never troublesome.
A childhood gift.
A childhood friend.
Received for Christmas or a birthday?
Can't remember.

He's in a cardboard box now,
waiting to be sent to his new owner in Africa.
Snuffles will soon be another expat!
Gifted to my baby grandnephew BK,
who will probably take better care of him than I ever did.

Are stuffed dogs meant for boys?
Are bunnies gender neutral?
I always preferred teddy bears.
Better than dolls,
except Saby (pronounced "Swaby").
My beautiful Black doll, the size of a baby.

I will never send her away!
Dolls! Parents insist girls love them.
Many of us eventually do.
We cuddle next to them.
Comb their silky hair, if they have any.

Saby does not!
It's just painted on.
At least most of our dolls were Black!
My oldest sister sewed outfits.
I never did.

What kind of a name is "Snuffles"?
Hanna-Barbera penned it for
an iconic cartoon character.
We loved HB and Snuffles,

a pesky bloodhound who
would do anything for a dog biscuit.
We all know people like that.

I never gave my Snuffles any biscuits.
He never begged me.
Perhaps I awarded some that were imaginary.

Such plaintive eyes. My only hound dog.
The best kind. He never cried.
Never needed veterinary shots.
Yes, he's old. Old like me.
But still ready to give and receive more love.

I washed him as best I could, so his stitches
would not become recalcitrant overnight.
Ears still floppy. A bit tattered.
His hearing may be shot.
Maybe a few patches will do?

Veterinarian still not needed.
Snuffles, give me another hug and kiss
before I close that demanding box.
Beforehand, I must take a few
parting snapshots of you.
Merci beaucoup! Bon voyage!

Era imprints sometimes fade gradually.
Pesky memories, even about Snuffles,
probably never will,
cause my Baby Boomer childhood
was toys, love, pride,
always buttressed by imagination   and reading.
Reading from our home library,
    Highlights for Children,   *Funk & Wagnalls*,   *Encyclopaedia Britannicas*,
      Ebony,   *Jet*,   and   *Life*   magazines,

we always had real paint to paint our lives.
Gordon Parks, one of my favorite painters,
will always remind us
that photographs are one way
we never have to say, "Goodbye."

Jif Peanut Butter

Wonder bread.
White.
Saltine crackers, easier to share.
Never saw sharp knives
in the kitchen. Hidden.
Always saw Cheerios
in our cupboards next to

Jif Peanut Butter
crunchy, sometimes creamy.
Slather on dollops, dollops of it
attempting to protect
thin jelly middles of kids
still learning to blend and blend.
Peanut butter stuck
to the roofs of
        Our mouths
            Our walls
                Our ceilings
                    Our homes
                        Our minds

while we cheerfully
asked for more.
Just tasted good
lasting all day while *They*

        called us *Negroes*
        years ago
        before
    our parents insisted
        we
        must
keep SunButter, wheat bread, and black pepper
    on our kitchen tables.

SNEAKERS

"I always wore sneakers when I wanted to. It was always about being comfortable and being myself."

—**Whoopi Goldberg**

2274 E. 74th Street

Fairfax Neighborhood. East Syde! Cleveland, Ohio. The beginning of *Me!* Lived there only seven years until we moved from our segregated neighborhood with segregated public schools where my teachers looked like *Me!* Where everybody looked like *Me!* Where *Desegregation* and *Integration* were foreign words. Cleveland still does not teach us how to speak them.

2274. Where gunshots in the distance didn't always disturb sleep. Where passing winos and derelicts was part of our homework. Inner City Blues? We four kids learned to feel safe. Most Black kids did back then. Even if our parents didn't.

2274. Our old house contained our family's heart. Lots of records, books, and magazines. Toys and Black dolls Mom made sure we loved. Always a Black and White television. Always a piano. Listening to Mom sing and play was also homework. Always more than one Bible.

2274. Our wide front porch with a metal glider. A favorite meeting place, second only to our back stoop where we put on plays and entertained ourselves in the open air. Third only to the kitchen table. The soggy Kellogg's corn flakes calling my name. Mom made me eat anyway before we kids walked to school together, so close seemed arm in arm. At night, blessing simple family dinners. We always ate together. Usually late, because Dad needed to dream longer.

2274. Other home productions. Sitting and getting my hair braided. Loved that London bridge of hair Mom used to plait just for me and Micki, because our hair was long enough for Mom's sculpting hands. Same chair where I first felt a howling-hot straightening comb against my scalp! Thank God, only on Easter Sunday and other special occasions.

2274. The place where I first looked at the world with my big, brown eyes. Peering into drawers. Always the little inspector. Bringing everything closer to my imaginary microscope. Carefully elevated on backyard swings other Black families could never afford. Me, thinking about big things, like how far away the clouds and open fields were. Wishing to reach both. If not that day, one day.

2274. The seeds of my myriad questions was planted there. Even future ones like, "Daddy, Patrice Lumumba. He has my middle name. Are they killing *everybody Black* named *Patrice*?" Dad, the *Captain of our Black History* and safety always allayed my fears. Our collective fears. He always had answers like hot chocolate with whipped cream. A favorite treat from nearby Howard Johnson's.

2274. Our parents' eager *Let's Move* conversations never really included us.

So we moved to a *better place* on the South-East Syde. Lee-Harvard where I had mainly White teachers. Some who quickly erased the words, Brown v. Education off their chalkboards. Some made us wish we could go back to segregated Fairfax. I walked home with a blonde classmate named Susan who had a Black maid.

Sue and I were *friends* until she moved to her own *better place*. Probably Shaker Heights. *Dream Suburb*. Liberals. Great schools still trying to strike out achievement gaps. To this day, "a model of integration." Historically, a national anomaly.

Only a baseball's throw away from our new home, previously owned by a Jewish family. *White Flight* became a cliché of the 60s. But the Nagys and Crandalls stayed. Lived right near us most of their lives. We even spoke to one another. Mr. Nagy gave us tomatoes from his backyard garden.

Only uncut grass remains on 2274. Our *Old House* had to be torn down years ago. My parents had paid off the mortgage long ago. Two homes paid in full! Old and new. Didn't have a "burn the mortgage party" like Archie and Edith Bunker. The fireworks in our Black parents' eyes were enough.

Mom's Hands
for my Mommy

Part 1

Knew, just knew how
to divide up one stick
of Wrigley's chewing gum
like we were all getting
fresh McDonald's french fries.
Gave everyone a little sip of decaf,
Maxwell House coffee in her cup.
We were adults sometimes, for a minute.

Bought us things, often on shoestrings,
dreaming about bigger pocketbooks.
Handed down hand-me-downs until
there were no hands left to hand down.
Handed us time to do homework
while she washed our dirty dishes by hand.

Loved her kitchen cause of us.
Taught three out of four well enough to take her spot.
No one ever made ice cream in the freezer like her.
Made an ice cube tray shiver with delight.
Vanilla always tasted better her way.

Left Tooth Fairy-dusted coins under our pillows,
even after we stopped believing.
Same with Christmas, Mom and Dad
gifting the best gifts any kid ever got.
Like Daphne, the biggest Black doll
we ever saw,
who could walk across our creaking wooden floors.

Studied the Bible,
prayed for us every day.
Folded up pocket prayers
she hid away with family secrets.
Dressed us to shine in church, school, libraries —
anywhere she felt we needed to glisten.
All the while teaching us how to listen.

Worked again
when an injury put Dad flat on his back.
Had three jobs then:
teacher, mother, wife.
Never too tired to love us all for life.

Part 2

Hands dropping sugar cubes into our lives.
Hands that always knew when to grasp the lemons.

That told the rolling pin how to make perfect biscuits.
That refused to let go of clothespins.
That still believed in scrubbing boards.
Ensuring the iron makes perfect creases.
Tying shoestrings and bows just right. Not too tight.
Flipping hoecakes in greasy cast iron skillets.
That separated the egg whites when we couldn't.
Sewing a gingham gym bag for one of us.
Dusting beloved horse figurines.
Refusing nail polish rule her throne.
Holding on to her purse like Queen Elizabeth.
Adjusting big safety pins, making space for growing waists.
A resting place for us.
Piano soulmates of Nina Simone and Nat King Cole.
Applying Oil of Olay to that one and only, remarkable face.
That held brown bags, flouring tasty fried drumsticks.
Straightening stubborn hair in the kitchen.
Braiding hair so it would never dare run.
That were never afraid to raise themselves at PTA meetings.
Adjusting church hats and gloves. Hers and ours.
Composing Kodak Brownie pictures at our picnics.
Carefully removing life's splinters from our fingers.
Guiding our bowling balls. Teaching us how to strike precisely.
Always folding more sheets for family.

Hands that still held mine when I was grown.
Hands in heaven never let go.

Sugar Cane and Green Beans
for my Daddy

Dad bought both at the Old Central Market. He knew we needed many more things to survive. Undeniably his favorite shopping spot, even after it closed. He went there many times, so proud to exchange his money for some happiness. Sugar cane and green beans.

The sugar cane stalks were cut, but still long. Green, sometimes pale green. We had to pull them off to get to the sweet middle. I always thought sugar cane was a fruit. Too sweet to be a vegetable. It's considered grass, and it grows and grows and grows.

Our Old Central Market green beans were always *fun!* More fun than playing in the forbidden streets. Have you ever snapped a green bean? That distinct, melodious sound.

Snap, snap, snapping away, never tiring of that mellifluous sound. A kind of sweetness even sweeter when we snapped in unison. A different sweetness than sugar cane, another chance for Daddy to see us in blissful unity.

Before we moved out of the ghetto, we used to put our beans in a bowl. Sit on our front porch on East 74th Street and snap them, one by one. We never snapped beans on the porch at the new house. Only indoors. Then less and less snapping and more and more canned or frozen choices.

Some of us have victory gardens now. While our ancestors never could. Daddy is smiling with them, knowing more of us will have our own gardens aplenty someday. Learn how to take whole foods and nourish our whole selves. Our bodies, minds, and souls. *Ashe!*

Haibun for Our Mothers' Gardens
for Alice Walker

When I was a kid, my mother tried to make me become Friends4Ever with weeds and grasshoppers. Meaning, because I was Louvenia Pugh's daughter, I was supposed to be that proverbial apple, not falling far from her tree. One of her nicknames for me was Louvenia Jr. so, if she could have made me her doppelganger, I'm sure she would have.

Sometimes, there were days when she would put on her garden gloves and kidnap me for at least thirty minutes. Call it part of my becoming a *woman?* Becoming a *future housewife?* Learning *to be at one with nature?*

Not exactly sure why she felt I must go outside to watch her every move. She did point out what was what each time. "What was what?" I said to myself. Never taking any written or mental notes. Mom was always my best teacher, but on the subject of gardening — to her chagrin and mine — I was asleep at my desk.

Green weed menaces were not menacing. Ones with the yellow and purple flowers were pretty. Never understood why they must be pulled. Then, banished to the trash can. "Mom, stop taking me on these terrifying foreign backyard safaris!" I said to myself. I sometimes even jumped higher than the largest grasshopper. He looked more like a lion to me!

Using her sixth sense, Mom knew I was restless. Thirsty for my kid canteen — whatever I considered fun to drink from it. Mom finally released me from captivity. Told me I could go play. Read or watch television. Practice my piano lessons. My sisters and I took lessons from Mrs. Kathleen Forbes. We were often sleeping at our desks in her class, too.

Black girls in gardens.
Mothers teach flowers. Colors.
Lavenders. Purples.

Ready

I remember asking, "When can I start wearing stockings?"
Kep' hearing.
"You are not ready."
"You are not ready."
"You are not Ready!"
"When can I wear a bra?"
Same answer.
"You are not ready."
"You are not ready."
"You are not Ready!"
"Not Ready!"
No need to ask about sex, the hidden question.
Why was my womanhood kept on a shelf?

In Christian households,
we already know the answers to certain questions,
because we've tacitly heard them before ever having to ask.
"Keep your legs shut and your nose clean!"
Never understood until guest speakers came to my high school.
Told us how women really get pregnant.
Was amazed it was not from dancing close in a basement while
listening to The Stylistics or Teddy.
More shocking was the news that storks didn't deliver babies!

So, I must be a cake waiting for the oven timer to sound?
We used to use that slow-rising flour, sometimes.
Any sudden disturbance made the cake droop —
then *drop!* before it was fully cooked.
So, the sad, sagged cake was edible,
but ruined for presentation.
All lopsided in the pan.
Not easy to remove either,
the bottom sticking.

Dribble
for BroWiley

Not sure why only *male* fireflies can fly. Still, fly.
Must be the physics of height and velocity.
Some men contemplate free throws in their sleep,
peak performances conditioned during embryonic stages.

Some women were once talented tomboys.
Girls, never heralded for Greatness.
Not with those names!
King James. Air Jordan. Black Mamba.
The Answer. The Truth.

Once upon a time, the pavements met our knees.
Scraped them. Consecrated them.
We got up for *Cocoa Butter* glories.
Bouncing so high, we touched maple-tree limbs.
Dunking over our baby brothers
and their friends.

Gurlz and Boyz
under streetlights together,
sometimes falling down.
Traveling.
Talking is *Treasure*. Not *Trash*.
Laughing about games.
Taking turns at free throws.
Respecting everyone's lanes.
Shooting hoops.
Hitting rims of hopes.
For Boyz   and   for Gurlz.

Fighting Back Four

All that nonviolent air in the 60s.
Kids still threw rocks at all of us.
Sometimes we had to throw bigger ones back,
but we were church people who carried
hand fans to ward off the heat,
knowing inside we needed something stronger,
but fans were all we had sometimes,
most of that time. Black moms and dads
made sure we wore the right clothes.
Shined the right shoes.
Especially at our schools.

Anthonette, aka Toni

Big sis tried to wear her
"revolutionary dress" to school one day.
Something Joni Mitchell, Odetta, or Joan Baez
might wear while strumming a guitar
singing Those Songs. Dress bright,
red and gold. High-waisted. Loose-fitting.
Bold. Too bold for Mom.

Mom and sis in the basement.
Sis pulled back.
Hootenanny dress was history.
Both might have laughed.
Mom might have hidden the dress,
but my sister never forgot.

They never repaired
the embattled wooden table
caught between them that day.
Sis never trekked to Woodstock.
But graduated from Kent State.
What happened four years before?
Ohio. Four died in Ohio.

Michelle, aka Micki

Second sis always knew how to fight.
Not sure why or how.
Her long, spindly fingers that played the piano
like she was in Carnegie Hall
also knew how to seize a foe's
hair, beat them down to the ground till
they had slow-to-heal bruises.
Knew how to claw and bite.
Her kid gloves and polished shoes
fooled them every time. So stealthy,
she could put to shame any combat soldier.

Marlana, aka Marti

Little girls like me never learned
to fight with their hands
like their sisters or brothers.
Little girls like me had older sisters
walking back to the school sidewalks with us,
our fingers reluctantly pointing out the culprit
who pushed us or said something bad about us.
Big sisters or Mom usually took care of the rest.
The enemy went home with skinned knees —
skinned egos or worse, depending on their resistance.

Years passed when I was always the first one
home from junior high. Missed all the big fights.
Heard the highlights like bellwork answers
in the first class daily.
My motto back then,
"I'd rather be called a chicken than fried ham."
Fighting with words most of my life,
most never put their hands on me.
Assumed harmless, another turnip
falling off the truck trying to be witty.
Now they know —
I can smoke their words without a gun.

Wiley, aka Tim, Baby Bro, BroWiley

Very little coaching needed cuz
Black men generally come out of the womb
swinging. Or singing. Baby Bro could do both.
Only used his fists as a last resort.
In high school, he fought
with one hand behind his back.
His mean adversary was handicapped.
My brother still won, but never bragged.
Baby Bro once fought, head-to-head,
with a glass door panel.
No surprise, he won.

Echoes of Richie Havens
and Gibson guitars,
Bro always used his voice
and hands to create love.
To create freedom.
Still in his youth, he became the
lead baritone in an integrated,
citywide group, The Singing Angels.
They spangled with Wayne Newton
at Nixon's first Inauguration.

 No weapons of mass destruction.
No militias with massive armored tanks.
No arsenals of guns in basements.
No aimless tear gas grenades ever thrown or landed our way.
The Four of Us? Our battles serious. Miniscule in the cosmos. The 1970s
shattered all of us. Watergate. Vietnam. Kent State. *Four dead in Ohio.**

Four dead in Ohio. Four dead in Ohio. How many more? How many more?

*Lyrics from "Ohio" written by Neil Young; sung by Crosby, Stills, Nash & Young

Mr. A. Leonard Jasper

He was the paternal grandad I never had.
I wish I had. I knew he was.
Better than the perfect stand-in.
Never a placeholder.

Lived two doors down.
With his wife, German shepherds,
and beloved backyard garden.
Filled with flourishing flowers
and sometimes rows of satisfied tomatoes.

Mr. A. Leonard Jasper. "A" for Austin which
suited him, a real gentleman.
Howard graduate with full-bodied
kindness and a sense of humor.
Boy Scout leader. Never a father,
but father to many boys like
Carl Stokes and Louis, his older brother.
Mr. J was grandad to girls like me who needed
more friends, such as confidence and levity.

Mr. A. Leonard Jasper. I will never forget him.
He let me eat orange sherbet ice cream.
A whole pint all by myself on his back porch.
On a very hot summer day.
He and his wife still had to coax me.
My parents? I would have been sharing
with one or two siblings. Most likely all three.

Years later, Mr. A. Leonard Jasper
gifted me, just me, Cross writing pens
before I realized I needed them.
Also passed down his passions
for nature and photography.

My oldest special friend from way back when
taught me the word, *Family*
has abundant elasticity. Yes, many times,
he showed me so does *Love*.

Milk Chute Queen

Back then when I was learnin bout SASSY,
never served any sassafras when I was young.

      Not me,   SLIM.   Some chose my stage name early.
                Thin and slippery as canola oily.
        Like one of those folks   with supple body parts
                        melding,
  bending easily   without breaking.   NOT   ANY BONES.
Contortionist?   **YEAH!**   I was a contortionist.

                Back then, my circus career seemed very short.
           All my next-door neighbors   named Hirsh ever needed
                   was a Temp.   **YEAH!**   Hired little me
                             temporarily   to slink through
                                           their milk chute
this time and that.   Like a snake or a cat.
Every time they   forgot   their keys.
With my parents' consent.
YEAH!   Always had to have that.

        Each time, someone gently lifted me by the knees
     while I magically shrank. Then maneuvered in arms first.
       To open the little inside door's latch while gingerly,
I PUSHED   PUSHED   PUSHED AWAY a few brooms and things in my way.

                   Voilá. Presto.
Took about a minute.
Felt like a gymnast. Stuck my landing again.
YEAH!   No team coach was ever in it.

              Opened the big side door.   The Hirshes entered.
           They always said eagerly,   "Thanks," to me.
              "What's a fitting reward for my temporary work?"
"A dime or a quarter."   I bought a Nestle's Crunch at my favorite drugstore.

                  Then I went outside.
         Kids and parents all buzzing round me.
     Handed me a scepter early. Looked like a BIG OL' trophy.
        Kids dressed me in a robe and paper crown.

Such a bedazzling display never found.
Sat on my PINK and BLUE throne.
Suddenly felt GROWN-GIRL-GROWN.
Officially, Queen Bee of Milk Chutes. Queen Bee of My Block.
YEAH!   I was never just *Slim* or just *Princess*.

Big Dreams

Palming big dreams like basketballs
in my little Black girl hands,
I wrote in my private workbook that I was *happy*.
Proud to write my *whole name* in *cursive*
with a Laddie pencil.
Navy blue. Very broad and thick back then.

9.5 years old in Grade 4B.
Already writing poetry in a coveted spiral notebook.
Drawing and painting the sky blue.
I sat up straight in class
spending days, months inside fountain pens
that seemed to last forever.
Never did. Some had replaceable cartridges.

I never dipped quills. Imagined it.
Musings resting and waiting in my inkwells,
screaming to flow out of my solitary chambers.
Me, sitting in a high, wooden seat somewhere ancient
where all the scribes can daydream.
Where we doff heavy, velvet robes and stylish berets.
No one dares to interrupt us having tea with our brains.

Before kid reality interrupts.
"Marlana, curve your hand to the right."
"Elevate your wrist, like this."
Miss Donna Hollinger, my White teacher,
at my little desk again.
Touching my pen hand.
Placing it *the right* way.
Trying to reshape not just my right
but my left, too.
Both my free hands following rules
felt like violation!

"Stop grasping the pen so low."
I never could form "k" that well.
Some days, my hand hurt from trying.
"Darn you, Zaner-Bloser *capital* letters!"
        "That elusive A+ in penmanship will one day be mine!"

Miss Hansen

Doing well in school is always my banner, so I never really need any captain besides me. I loved school even before school started. My parents always helped steer in many unique ways back then, so did Miss Hansen.

Miss Hansen was my sixth-grade teacher, our MTV Star before MTV! She clapped, sang, and danced around our classroom in her open-toed flat shoes. Her bargain basement dresses on her tall, slender frame. Her mousy gray hair slightly above her shoulders made her look like someone's forgotten aunt or aging rock star. She looked pixilated, but that was her passion showing. Genius mistaken for craziness.

She was crazy enough to make herself unforgettable to all her students. She rhymed like Eminem. Macklemore. Machine Gun Kelly. Possibly better considering the times, her fervor, and rapt audience. "Fifty. Sixty. Seventy. Eighty. Time to Practice Multiplication Tables!" Teaching us two for the price of one skills, she found clever ways to incorporate her rhyming into our math and other lessons.

Yes, she was White. Many of our teachers were SWFs back then. She was a "Spinster." That was the term then. We students were all her kids regardless of our colors. We were her family along with her aging mother. Miss H was devoted to us all who were mostly Black. An *Ally* before it was cool to say she loved us. Before the kumbayas came with our MLK National Holiday. Before Black History Month was openly celebrated. Before Whites started applauding that Black is Beautiful and that our lives matter. Before cultures got canceled again, Miss Hansen had our whole class read about George Washington Carver. A whole book. We had discussions.

One other vivid memory remains. One day, she walked up to my desk. We had assigned flip top desks where we could store most of our young lives. Our books, pencils, papers, crayons, and other school essentials. She supplied the paint and extra paper for our art classes. Miss Hansen who taught us every subject that year, including some beginning French, walked over to my desk, leaned down, then softly said without measuring any words,

Why are the people in your picture, **Orange?**

I really did not have an answer. I had been drawing as well as painting **Orange** people for quite some time. I guess one could say **Orange** was a good blend of *White* with *Brown* plus darker shades. Looking sun-tanned was a happy medium.

Guess what Miss Hansen said?
"You should make your people, Brown! Understand?"

I just nodded my head, in agreement, not in obedience. We loved her, so I did not consider her suggestion as an insult. One that meant I had no right to draw or paint **Orange** people. From that day forward, no one had to ask me about **Orange People** anymore!

Call Mrs. Frances Mason Franklin
for Carol

At Charles W. Eliot Junior High,
Mrs. Franklin walked into any room,
every child took their seat.
Made adults want to sit up straight.
Not squirm or speak.

Might be very busy teaching her own class.
When alerted, Mrs. Franklin
made arrangements to assist very fast.
Armed with her hose, standing
five feet nothing with a whole lot of everything.
With a flip of one hand, she put out classroom fires
all over our school building.

That bullhorn at her hip hoisted daily so deftly
front center, Mrs. Frances Mason Franklin,
a Black lady not scared of anyone or anything.
Not even a thousand voices yelling in one primal scream.
A legend before Joe Louis Clark ever picked up any bat.
Clark's bullhorn probably took lessons from hers!

Principal Sokol knew he needed her to step in.
"Call Mrs. Frances Mason Franklin. Call her!"
She had teachers and parents,
everyone wanting to unlock mysteries.
Wanting in-depth interviews late after school.

Will never forget how it felt
when she walked into a room.
Our Pied Piper. Our classroom whisperer.
An English teacher who could teach Shakespeare
and Langston Hughes, with or without textbooks.
Spelman graduate who put you in a learning spell.
No more running from knowledge.
She had student after student begging
for her help getting into college.
"Please. Please, call Mrs. Frances Mason Franklin!"

Finding Our Tar Beaches
for Faith Ringgold

Mother, after migrating to Cleveland,
why didn't you ever make a quilt just for me?
Patchwork with jack-o'-lanterns and horses,
stories we can truly see?

Running, rubbing fingers over uneven threads,
wishing. Wishing. Wishing
the panels and stitches came from our heads.
Not another's. Octogenarian with talent
passed down in Gee's Bend
or Charleston, S. Cee.

Color notwithstanding, another person,
not family preserving, recording.
Then what becomes of you and me?
Our posterity?

Buying quilts at Walmart, Kmart, Etsy.
Mother, Mother, is this how it has to be?
Up North, disposing of our hearts.
Appropriating, not perpetuating our legacies.

Christmas Wrapping Paper and Bows
for my sister, Michelle

Christmas firesides not blazing bright.
Not for the homeless.
Not for the unhappy.
Our fires back then
never smoked up Santa's chimney.
Coal came down a basement chute
at the old house.
New home on Talford
registered heat from a big,
sometimes bellowing furnace.
Warmed by snug floor vents
open wide in December.

Just like our desires, our dreams
to always stay like that together.
To keep Santa alive and Toll House
cookies in the oven
longer than December. Longer than life.
White or Black Santa?
White or Black Jesus?
Kids believing in tearing open
wrapped trucks, bikes, Barbies,
they did not care. It did not matter,
not like now.
Smiles were all.
Merry Christmas — two good words.

Wrapping paper everywhere.
Adults still making kid bets. Micki and I.
Our fun, silly wrapping contests
started after our own kid coins
laughed and bought gifts.
Gave us permission.
Win. Lose. Draw. No matter.
Packages dressed up.
Colorful bows brimmed over wrapping paper.

An unwatched holiday pot
of black-eyed peas seasoned just right
with our delicious love for one another.

Families under once-real pine trees
shedding needles. Discarded now,
aluminum tree replacements
stored in attics,
joyously decorated together,
hoping, praying our Christmases as sisters,
as family, would last forever.

Joy to Our World

Singing *Joy to the World* in three-part harmony
easier than piano lessons on Saturdays,
building the perfect snowman,
or layering right before going outside.

Mom's soaring soprano used to leading.
Her four lambs learned to sing in our sleep.
Patty next door and others.
Our friends not trained singers, but family.
We all aimed to please Mom that eve.

Caroling *O Holy Night* first,
our homes heard us singing.
Hats and scarves already fully rehearsed.
Smooth a capella sounds.
We Three Kings were sleds
snuggling our knees and cold noses.
Mittens, gloves knew every song's verses.
Voices melding melted muddy ice,
defogged resisting window panes,
cold drafts and shovels stopped.

               LISTEN.

          Persistence guided our boots.
          What Child Is This? had to be sung.
          Under the last approving streetlight,
          Silent Night made everything still.
          Calmed everyone's blended voices.

Hot chocolate and popcorn
applauded our singing inside.
Asked for encores.
Mom's Spinet piano chords.
Our voices much louder,
much warmer than our thick socks,
    sang *Joy to the World* again.   Then again.   Then again.

AmeriVision
for Gil Scott-Heron

We Boomers grew up with AmeriVision —
the ability to see numerous one-dimensions,
pretending the fake is actually real.
Your Amoses, your Andies,
your Beulahs,
your Stepin Fetchits,
your "Yes, boss" chauffeurs,
your "Yes, ma'am" maids.
Saw all of them on our living room screens,
the ones on our streets we call that name, "Uncle Tom."

Watched *The Little Rascals* regularly,
right after cartoons,
knowing Mighty Mouse and Rocky the Flying Squirrel are not real,
just cartoon characters able to overcome heavy anvils on their heads,
be riddled with bullets,
pop up like *Jiffy Pop*. Rejuvenated. Never dead!
The Little Rascals, integrated cast of little kids.
Could be our neighborhood playmates.
Darla, Alfalfa, Stymie, and Buckwheat —
that whole gang of innocent innocence.
As a kid, I never thought about it seriously. Not then.

Until protests became a big word.
Became BREAKING NEWS!
DISTURBING NEWS!
TEARFUL! TERRIFYING! NEWS!
Worse than King Kong pummeling skyscrapers
or kidnapping a screaming Fay Wray on our screens.
I never marched with King or Evers.
I never met George Wallace or Barry Goldwater.
But I did see all of them on TeleVision!

My family and I felt it.
Black America felt it, even on our screens,
which were no longer real filters.
Felt the police-trained German Shepherds

snapping, salivating,
eager to bite knees of women and children.
Water hoses attached to gushing fire hydrants,
knocking our dignified Black hands,
filled with purpose, to the ground.
Feeling unspeakable hurt and shame.
Over and over again!
Saw assassinations, then funerals TeleVised.
Fine Black and White pillars of our nation dying young.
America can never forget TeleVision and VIETNAM!

Turn off our screens!
Lose all the filters!
Leave all America's Tunnel Visions behind us!

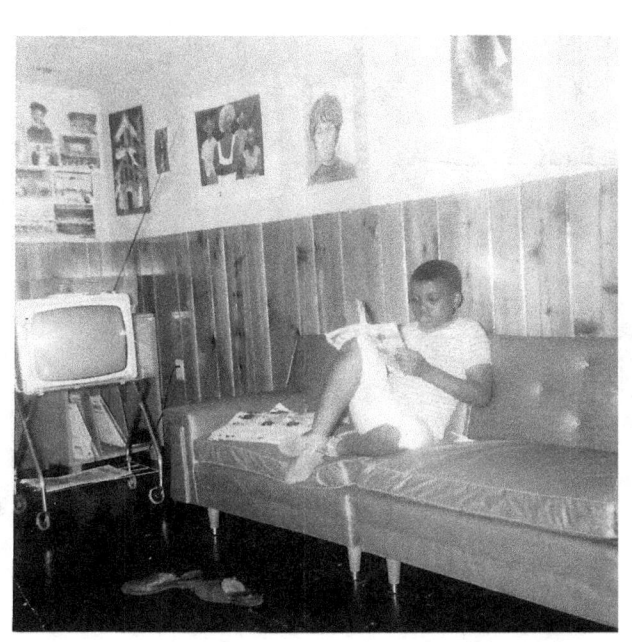

BLACK & WHITE SADDLE SHOES

"What confines, impoverishes, exploits, enslaves, oppresses, sickens, bloodies, rapes, and kills women are not generally clothes or shoes, but rather laws and societal norms."

—**Summer Brennan,** *High Heel*

The Ballad of Annie: Just Another Media Event

October, 1960. Harvard-Lee.
We were the tree-lined, the Black Bourgeoisie.
Maples shaded short skips from churches, stores, schools.
Evergreens waved us across streets.
Oaks encouraged obedience
under their coolness.
Annie enticed boys,
provoked fights,
baited nice girls like me.
Annie was the girl across the street who
never became my friend.
Weren't enemies.
Just never friends.

We grew up in the same tree-lined neighborhood, then grew apart.
Never said Annie was bad
or I was better.
She was wilder
than wild olive trees!
Long before puberty,
Annie just had better things to do.
Gossiping. Ridiculing. Intimidating four-eyed smart girls like me
who pleased parents rather than ourselves.
Preparing for more cleanliness —
clean families, clean jobs, clean money.

While many chose to read college books under cool shade trees,
Annie prepared for more conquests.
Popular Annie knew how to look cute and be tough.
Kissing boys was the only homework that put her on top.
Year after year, some of our neighborhood trees
became hardened and broken
with no one there to graft them.

July, 1992. Harvard-Lee.
Our Buckeye obstructed the bedroom view.
Visiting, aided by binoculars, I still saw IT.
DRUG TASK FORCE emblazoned on T-shirts across the street.

INTERLOPERS knocking holes in walls in my old
neighborhood!

A street party forming without the music blaring.
Noise of the new INVADERS on Annie's front lawn.
Spilling outward with children on bikes,
a minister, the councilman feigning concern
for the Channel 43 reporter with his video crew.
Annie's fruit, her young son, overwhelmed.
Rescued by his Aunt Shirley, the good one.
Rescued at least for a day.
Our tree-lined street deeply disturbed now.
Cordoned off for countless hours.
Lined with police cars!

Cameras ready as Annie emerges from the house
across the street in
MANACLES!
Someone from our neighborhood in MANACLES!
Cuffs secure behind her back.
She was a daze of dishevelment with escorts, not the kind she wanted.
Looked like her brother who had just returned from prison.
No wig or leather holding her together.
She was BALD!
A forty-year-old hussy attempting some dignity too late,
Annie crouched from embarrassment.
Hid from the vacuousness
and her confused son.

After her parents' deaths, even before,
Annie had welcomed the horns,
the visitors' honks at midnight.
Condoms. Paraphernalia was the unspeakable kind of sprawl
lying spread-eagled in our tree-lined neighborhood.
The Black Bourgeoisie
and their trees have disappeared.
Some rotted. Some cleared.
I wonder. Still wonder.
          "Why do trees with firm roots clutching the earth still rot?"

Coretta

I am sure you had a garden,
a lush one in Atlanta.
Women like you always do.
At dusk, you and Martin strolled there admiring the lilies.
The only times you had moments like that together, without haste.
Tending your flowers alone,
you wore your favorite garden gloves and apron. Sun hat.
Sometimes barehanded to feel the soil, like new dough,
and even the stickers to remember the pricks.
I imagine you filled your home with fresh sunflowers
on the dinner table where Martin sometimes met with others.
Ministers' wives know all about that,
and ironing shirts, straightening ties,
and fitting cufflinks for final passages.
Making lunches. Long days at church and Sunday dinners.
Long walks down Memphis streets with Martin.
You were prepared for all of that.
April 1968, you learned quickly.
We watched on television.
So admired on that famous *Ebony* cover,
Coretta taught children,
especially daughters, how to become women, wives, and mothers.
Coretta, forever our queen mother.

Sacristan

Most times, we learn to carry what is written on our clothes, even if we'd rather cut out the labels scraping at the napes of our necks. Sometimes, we purposely destroy them. Sometimes, the labels just get lost or wear off. Sometimes, the labels never go away, because that's how society likes it. Sometimes, the labels are our destiny.

In high school, we wore uniforms, so my attributes and expectations were always in full view: Young. Black. Woman. Tall. Slender. Ambitious. Smart. Overachiever. Collegiate. Neat. Kind. Ladylike. Respectful. Quiet. Shy. Loner. Writer. Actress. Entertainer. Virgin.

Non-Catholic.

Non-Catholic!

Not being Catholic attending an integrated Catholic high school for girls.
Vowing to fit into their cogs without changing mine.
To this day, I am AME, African Methodist Episcopal,
the denomination that fits me. Most of my family. Our ancestors.
Never wanted to kiss anyone's ring.
Never wanted to call any man "Father" except my own.
Never wanted to carry my religion on my back.
Never wanted to marry my religion, just a kind Black man.

On our school Mass days, we opened our veins
for the Anglo-Saxon rituals.
To worship in scaled-down splendor.
Most of our *Nuns* were still *Nuns*.
Most of our *Priests* were still *Priests*.
Our *Priests* were assisted by *Sacristans*.
This *Overachiever* became one.

Loved still love hearing the Latin I will never understand.
Hands in unison signing the cross.
The holy water sprinkled.
The Hail Marys for one special woman.
The raiments reserved and adorned only on the men.

Even the confessionals run by them.
The tinkling of that special bell. Sometimes my job.
The genuflects for the Holy Host.
The bejeweled, heavy chalices never meant for me.
Sacristan, a hallowed label once mine.

Blonde

Used to stare at this senior in my Advanced Biology class.
Not albino, but the next shade of pale. Everything.
Her hair.
Her skin.
Even her personality.
Aryan in intricate detail.
Every day, I would gaze.
My seat assignment put me in perfect alignment,
perpendicular to her
whether I liked it or not.
She was there, in front of me, every single day.
I wanted to look away.
Having to see her disturbed me.
But now I realize I never wanted her—
maybe I just wanted to be her.
We were never friends.
She was not more special or smarter than I was,
a junior among all those seniors.
If we ever conversed, it was not memorable.
She was just intriguing in a textbook definition,
Brigitte Bardot, Cate Blanchett, Nicole Kidman,
Tilda Swinton alabaster kind of way.
I do not even remember that girl's name,
but I remember her face,
just like we all remember Barbie dolls
when we check out our cellulite in a full-length mirror.
Not the Black version.
I am talking about the original Barbie.

Prototypes and Goddesses. There was only one Marilyn Monroe.
Not Madonna, Pamela, Chistina, Jessica, or, may she rest, Anna Nicole Smith.
Anyone who revered Marilyn knows she was dumb smart.
Worked perception to her advantage —
and tragic disadvantage.
Theories lingering about her death.
To this day, it amazes me how many White women love to say,
"I'm having a blonde moment."
Even the peroxides know *dumb* is a badge of achievement.

Morrison's *The Bluest Eye* explains everything.
What makes women of color still straighten their hair
or bleach their skin
or dislike being called *Dark, Midnight,* or *Ashy?*
Why was only one Spice Girl crowned *Scary?*
Why does confidence now mean *Diva?*
Why does strong and single lead to self-hatred?

It's been years of identities fought for and finally achieved.
That's all of us.
But Black women and their hair.
That's David battling Goliath with boiled oil and blow torches.
Cantilevers and catapults.
India cautions everybody that "I Am Not My Hair."
I agree, least to say my hair is not my spirit.
Or is it?

At the salon, I always dread a cut, even ends trimmed.
It's like part of my essence is getting ready to be swept into the trash.
Like Samson, I am reduced.
In America, less hair is less beauty.
Big chops? Baldness?
For men and cancer patients —
not the masses.

I know a young biracial girl who is an anomaly.
Happy and proud of her nickname, *Nappy.*
No way does she consider herself *MixedUp* or a *Zebra.*
On the other end, a little dye and weave,
far too many of us are perceived
Ghetto Fabulous.
Famous for rockin' hairstyles and clothing —
but never books.

My Black & White Saddle Shoes

Often part of my daily uniform
Hoban Dominican High School.
Knee socks, black or gray.
Regulation dress code.
Skirt lengths measured.
Too many inches
above the knee a crime.
Some of our fastest girls
walked that plank with pride.
Wearing black and white saddle shoes!

Uniforms kept us from raising ruckuses
(or so our White nuns thought).

I was a little puppy, willing
to roll over on command —
at least I let them think so.
Even if we all dressed alike,
trust had to be earned.

Thought I had when I won!
The Neatness Award.
If you ever wore a uniform,
you understand.
Winning that prize
was like winning an Academy Award.
No acceptance speech.
But names were called for each winner.
I stood and bowed.
May have done a beauty pageant wave.

Wool uniforms worn daily
start to STINK.
Dry-cleaning bills once a month,
not every week.
Out-of-uniform days.
Imagining ourselves as regular school kids,
but more special.

Collegiate. Our version of *Preppy*.
Cardigan sweaters everywhere.
On our shoulders. But never around waists!
Still had restrictions on what we could
and could not wear.
Hoban was educating young ladies.
Not *Hooligans*.

Three years of feeling like I was
suiting up for the army had me wanting
to hurl my saddle shoes out the nearest pristine window.
Did not burn anything in a trash can.
Some probably did.
One shred her pleated, plaid skirt
like a hula skirt.
Ran it up our flagpole.
We cheered and then ran.
Those nuns almost had us
fingerprinted for that.

Actually kept my saddle shoes
for their style and simplicity.
As a remembrance.
Reminding me never again
to be saddled like that anymore.
The uniform and shoes looked great on me.
Not false *camaraderie*, *unity*, and *pride*
spelled out in school handbooks
our nuns insisted we study. Even MEME-OR-IZE.

Years later, wore my shoes again.
A Throwback School Spirit Day at work.
Nostalgia's serenade enthralled
me one last day.
Never again?
My black and white saddle shoes are in a box now,
pushed way, way back in my closet
where they can be silent.

White Cotillion Dresses

Young Black daughters in *White* cotillion dresses
should be accepted everywhere.
Into any suburb, chalet, five-star restaurant.
Passing for *White*.
Dating *White*.
Marrying *White*.
At least the *Light-Skinned* passed brown bag tests.
No bleaching creams will remedy various shades of melanin.
The absence of *White*, silky skin.
Reality always trumps pretense.

Black girls without debuts in *White* cotillion dresses,
still sitting there with the latest *Call & Post*,
publisher a rich, Black Republican. W. O. Walker.
A man whose suit pockets knew how to please.
Attract more and more beautiful, Black bees to those hives.
Even if Daddy never went to Harvard or Morehouse,
never got a diploma —
made ball bearings at GM.

But each week, Black high-society pages awakened
every Black girl's imaginations.
Their Dads seated with them, with those others.
Their college degrees across
broad *White* tuxedo chests.
Waiting to see us in our billowing
White cotillion dresses.
White centerpieces. *White* corsages.
White nosegays. *White* boutonnieres.
White gloves pressed to lengthy perfection.
Escorted by proud, pencil-thin young Black men
who will probably go to Hampton or Fisk in the fall
with help from the *United Negro College Fund*.

Matriculating at Spelman, Howard,
or other HBCUs. For at least four years,
honey dreams fulfilled mainly for *Your People*.

One day, police harass,
then arrest, some Black father, Dr. Skip Gates
in his own *White* neighborhood
where some keep saying Blacks
with degrees don't even know how
to recycle bottles and cans.
Not even in The Inkwell.
Don't belong in Shaker Heights either.
A so-called model of integration.
Go back to strictly Section 8 housing!

Young Black daughters,
take off the *White* debutante dresses
worn over and over.
Those long *White* gloves.
White pearls strangling you.
None will ever prepare you
for *White Nooses!*

Jeez Louise!

The Bride of Frankenstein.
Frightened hair suited me then.
Afraid to speak words
that my parents
and religious admonitions
attempted to scare
out of existence.
The electric shocks of disapproval
coursing deep into my brain.
Every red corpuscle inside
silently screaming for more oxygen.
We Black young ladies were upright.
Learned early to sing
and play the right tunes on our pianos.
Not really me,
just who I was then
on the Halloween days
of my Black-girl youth,
still searching. Waiting to
fill my swirling magic bag.

I never swore outright back then.
Not until years later, when
someone made me take off my
passive-aggressive resting face.
Until then, *Jeez Louise!* suited
my well-flossed vocabulary perfectly.

Was a "White girl in Catholic high school" phrase
more popular than *Gee Whillikers!*
Holy Toledo! Gosh Darnit!
Countless other silly euphemisms.
Jeez Louise! had more panache.
Sounded mysterious, almost French,
like when they say, *Mon Dieu!*
My Black classmates and I became parrots, obsessed,
repeating just out of habit.

Said *Jeez Louise!* without any hesitation,
forever rolling those tasty words
off our tongues.
Who were we fooling?
We were not French, European, or White!

Just guilty.
Guilty as charged with the crime,
Assimilation.

Not that heinous one,
Cultural Appropriation.
Just a fancy name for what?
Is it *Them*, not Us?
Thief, hijacker, wannabe, pretender?

Don't want Vanilla Ice cream clones.
Don't want Bo Derek braids trending.

      Jeez Louise!   *Jeez Louise!*   *Jeez Louise!*

That Adrian Dominican Nun

Catholic High School   Hurt,   *Harmed*,   WOUNDED ME!
Angers me why that one teacher
never spoke to me. Never really saw me.
That nun. Order of Adrian Dominican Sisters.
A young White woman
neatly dressed in her updated white,
trimmed in black habit. Rosary at her side.
Friendly teacher smile.
Never kept her from her diabolical habit
when she and I were all alone in any hallways.

That nun did it purposely. I refuse to mention her name on purpose.
Suffice to say, the one who taught American History.
All about truths and slavery.
I should have been grateful like
the rest of her "privileged" Black students.
Hoban Dominican High students: 96% Catholic.   50% integrated.
The "Black Chosen" integrated into that building
filled with human relics, not just statues.
Black girls blending in so well with the plaster.

Did I need to be this sister's eternal sycophant?
Did I need to build her a throne?
Because she pretended she saw me in class.
Heard my voice. Tolerated me. The smartest
Black girl she might ever pretend to see?
Other White nuns were prejudiced,
but most never rowed their boats of hatred
back and forth from the River Styx. Not like she did.

Sister never spoke to me alone in any hallways!
Just glared in my direction.
Judging and fearing my every thought. My every movement.
Every single excellent grade and academic improvement I made
like I was bringing poisons to Hoban High daily
concealed inside my beloved books and loose leaf binders
intending to destroy all that she and others held sacred.

Her refusals to even say "Hello" then taught me how subterfuge
actually works in this world.
She could shave me away like pencil lead
in a sharpener every school day after school day.   Then confess and pray.
No classmates suspected or knew.
They worshipped God, the Virgin Mary,
the priests, the nuns, especially her.
No one else knew how her *Eyes*,
her *White Gaze* disdained me. Disrespected me.
Only I knew.   Only God knew.   Now you know about nuns like her.

Big Daddy

Big Daddy had eyebrows that could smile
and dance above his head,
hairless and smooth.
Arched and so dark looking drawn on his face.
Handsome as his suspenders
dependably framing ampleness.
Mom's father was
Clinton Gillispie (not Gillespie)
from Meridian, Mississippi!!!
Calling him "Big Daddy" and Grandma, "Big Momma" or "Big Ma."
Names that stuck like molasses on pancakes.

Big Daddy always so animated chiding us for not eating enough:
"Settle down.   Gone EAT! We ALWAYS have PLENTY."
Paraphrasing what he used to tell his grandchildren at Christmas gatherings.
There's a famous HAPPY Family Photo.
Kids seated in front.
Adults and baby in the back.
We were all smiling, especially Big Daddy.

We always smiled as we ate
Fried Chicken,   Collard Greens seasoned with   Pork and Chitlins'
             with mandatory Hot Sauce, Cornbread,
                              Dee-li-cious Macaroni and Cheese.
                   crunched, tickled our throats.
Dee-Light going down.

Seconds? Such is inward joy.
Scooping out love from
overcooked edges of Big Ma's pans.
Kissing robust kisses.
Goodbye hugs and snugs.
His proud expanding middle
always smiling belying Regrets.

Big Daddy's funeral was filled with favorite hymns.
promises and tears.
Also some buckets of embarrassment.

Served by one relative in the pew
wailing nonsense
about not being able to serve him another meal.
Claiming she cooked his last one.
If anyone had, it was only Big Ma.

        Promised 3 Score and 10.   Blame and grief are often twins.
Diabetes coupled with complications.   Big Daddy was only 61.
                Gone. So *Old* to me then.

75

My First Sea of Misogyny

I was the only girl in the car.
Driving Class.
Auto simulations in the trailer.
Car crashes if your pedal is not to the metal. Check.
Not real. Fake scary.
Followed by riding
in the real car with a
male instructor.
Far Scarier!
Let's call him **Mr. Black**.
Me with just boys, **Black**.
Usually, two or three.
With **Mr. Black**, **Black** Driving Teacher.

I drowned every time.
No one there to pull me
back into the lifeboat.
They heard me gurgling.
Voices always pushing
my self-confidence
back into the water,
Mr. Black enjoyed submerging me.

Never allowing me.
Could not even help me make a right turn,
dismissed to the back seat
watching all of that
TESTOSTERONE victoriously taking the wheel,
cheering on the all-male **Black** team
winning all his swimming trophies effortlessly.

Not even one for   a   terrified 17-year-old   **BLACK GIRL**
just   trying
to

drive
dive into

MEEEEEEEEEEE

MEEEEEEE

MEEEEE

MEEE

MEE

ME

They never saw

ME!

Never forgetting   my first sea   sea of misogyny.

Promgate

In 1973, the Watergate trials were on all summer.
Stupidity and sheer ineptitude pre-empted
all our favorite afternoon shows.
Wish those trials had pre-empted
my trials. My embarrassments.
One of them I call, Promgate.

At an all-girl's high school,
we had to do that Sadie Hawkins thing.
All the time asking boys if they
want to take us somewhere. Do something.
Permission was not a pointless word then.

At least I went to the Harvest Ball.
Our name for the Junior Prom.
That packaged photo is stored
in my proof of life bin.
Still have my pink lace dress.
If I kept my corsage, I cannot tell you.
Mom had taught us how
to press old flowers into wax paper
Always forgot to label the happy ones.

My silver shoes with low square heels long gone.
No high heels or I would have
towered over Richard, my date.
Nice enough looking. Smart enough.
He and I had kissed once in the music room
while watching TV. First awkward kiss.
Never kissed him again.
Imagined he could become my husband.

Instead, Richard was only my Harvest date.
One date harvested by our moms.
Could not pry off his jelly jar lid again.
He said, "No,"
when I asked him last-minute to take
me to the prom. His prerogative.

No last-minute Lucy.
I had my filmy blue dress from Winkelman's.
Might have bought it on sale.
Blue matching shoes. Both returnable.
Barry from Benedictine said he'd take me.
My first and only high school boyfriend.
Told me early!
Made me finally feel like I was a girl
ready to do what other girls
probably already did.

I believed him. Told supposed-female friends.
Then disbelieved Barry when
he backed his promise into a back alley. Acted like he did not know me.
Treated me like a clown wearing too much red lipstick.

I believe Jealousy prompted the cat burglary.
Some female, possibly with thirsty accomplices,
came in the night and stole Barry's promise
right out of my bedroom closet.
Probably laughed in the process.
Might as well have taken my dress and shoes.
Taken my trusting nature with them.

To this day, I cannot identify
any of the culprits.
Indistinguishable faces of classmates
waiting to discourage him. To slight me.
Jealousy? Just suspects.
To this day, no one has ever been convicted.
No guilty party has confessed.

Baptisms, birthday parties, graduations.
Proms. Dating. Losing virginity. Weddings.
Motherhood. Hysterectomies. Divorces. Deaths.
Embarrassments. Disappointments.
The order has no order anymore.

Women's rites of passage can become
unlawful rights to be excluded. Humiliated. Violated.
After cold cases are closed
due to lack of leads and evidence,
we women still see the residue in our bedroom closets.
On our bathroom mirrors and sinks.
In the bathtub. On the sofa
where we finally fall asleep.
Can we forget painful memories etched on our bedposts?
Promgate. I will always remember.

Possessions

Past 7:00.
Men in sun visors and brown suit coats
procrastinate
in shoes needing new heels.
Sporting, bopping, stopping at the Convenient.
Across Cedar, or Shell on Chester.
The machine will pop jaws shut at 7:30 sharp!
Sharper than these men will ever be.

Calling out numbers like speaking in tongues.
"Give me 411 straight... And boxed... Wheel it...
A kicker, too..."
"Regulars okay. The rest must write them down."
Lists jitterbugging lists filled with
Digits, Digits, Digits...

Shielded by the plastic partition
fogged with breath, dirt,
and
dreams,
the cashier blows her stale bubblegum.
Pops it in unison with the machine.
Then twirls the last slips of redemption
onto the turntable.

The Protest That Never Happened

The Book: *The Adventures of Huckleberry Finn*. Required reading assignment.

The Author: Mark Twain, revered American novelist and humorist.

The Place: John Carroll University, suburban Jesuit university with White female students with foreign American names like *Muffy*. Probably in college for their M.R.S. Almost 0% diversity, faculty and students alike.

The Time: Circa 1970s, when some Black folks wore their pride as window dressing.

The Professor: Dr. M, a White liberal who eventually married a Black woman. In his defense, he did not pick the required reading. Do not kill the messenger? He did bring Gwendolyn Brooks to our campus!

The Course: Freshman English 101, required for those who did not score high enough on the SAT Verbal.

The Students: Predominantly White with Black tokens on scholarships, grants and loans. Barely making it on money parents did not have, but found through overtime driving taxis and working double shifts.

Code Words: No messing up or being put on academic probation!

The Protest: The N-word used repeatedly in the text. 214 times! 71 out of 230 pages. 31% of the novel. The character Jim, a stereotype we want to bury in a bottomless pit, along with some of our shiftless American forefathers.

The Would-Be Protestors: Less than a handful of Black students. The leader, a lukewarm rabble-rouser who probably read the book, but only saw the N-words. A Black female. About 25. Old. Not worried like the rest of us, so fresh. Probably egged on by the Black Student Union. They had their own table in the cafeteria. Our parents said don't sit with the BSU. What a concept, segregating from the segregated.

The Verdict: Do not break *Their* rules. Just read the novel (or pretend   you   did). Many felt lucky to be at that school.

The Retrospection: Don't count those words. Read the book!

Haiban for Mr. Cotter, Blessed English Teacher

Clean cut. Crew cut. Well-cut neutral suits with white pocket squares folded. Neatly. Precisely. Taught at Harvard. Looked like Harvard. Nothing distracting. Nothing distracting about insisting we write in blue books. Nothing distracting about the dizzying way he talked to us. Spoke to us, John Carroll students. For 35 years! No distractions dare enter his classroom. Every student knew, "Always be punctual." Even though he always seemed kind, there was something that said, "Never disappoint me. Never spell, SORRY."

That Socratic Method. HIS Socratic Method gifted us with Big Thoughts. Mind-blowing questions. Daily! Almost BURSTING OUT classroom windows. We always left the door closed so nothing TOO BRILLIANT escaped into the hallway where others might not understand all that hydrogen. All that verbal combustion. Our labial jousting and wordplay made my head hurt, sometimes. But in a good way. All the possibilities. All the outcomes. White students and Blacks, usually one, me speaking while equal opportunities sat in the classroom with us.

Discussions with a White teacher about things that MATTERED or might not matter if you weren't an English major. Who cares about *The Emperor Jones, A Streetcar Named Desire*, or *Death of a Salesman*? Mr. Cotter made us care about ALL OUR FAMILIES. Made us talk candidly. This blessed teacher secretly realigned minds using constellations while on the campus at night. Then gave us the how-to-manual during his daytime classes, making the impossible positively palatable. Making us long for his kaleidoscopes to be in pockets everywhere. I gladly chased the clock to his class every day. He usually rewarded me with an A. He had presence of mind in every way to ELEVATE ALL.

Chase dreams to summits.
Keep meteors marveling.
Inhale majesty.

Ray Midnight

Ray, I still almost see you.
Your high school nickname, *Midnight*.
Imperfect Afro, green field jacket, granny glasses.
A young Curtis Mayfield?
Taller.
More swag.
Yep, your *Pimp Walk* was swag in a bottle.
Leading to your demise.
Too much *Rage*.
Too much *Rhetoric*.
Too many *Revolution* coils to uncoil.

When you spoke in the cold,
your words compelled us to shiver.
To change our bourgeois ways?
To love your words.
Your thoughts captivating, at least as long as we were on the bus riding with you.
When we got off that bus to walk in step through the briskness,
your words would always circle in the wind,
around your heavy head and ours.
Then that bluster trailed under you like dead oak leaves on the ground.
Once we reached Kulas Hall, we all scattered.
Scurried to separate classes where each of us
was usually *The Only One*.

Words often lead us to both progress and distress.
Word is, you called a Priest an ineffable name!
One that got you shoved to the floor
while the rest of us were looking at college doors.
Word is, you had a mental breakdown.
Word is, you worked at a gas station
or kept being seen at one near where she lived.

Word is, you killed that *White Woman* who lived
in an apartment overlooking Shaker Square.
Did you think she was your Desdemona?
Word is, your distinct *Walk* was part of the defense against you.
The fact is, you were convicted. Imprisoned.

Are you another locked-up *Innocent*? Or tragically guilty *Bigger Thomas*?
Are you dead now? If not physically, how about mentally?
Would you remember me?
Still remember you.
The fact is, I used to write many times in my diary.
About you and *Me*! About just *you*!
Another Black man with ideas.
Once a friend, dreaming *Midnight* dreams.
Creating other dreamers begetting more dreams.
Another Black man forced to become *Midnight* again.

My Michael

Called *Different*,
reduced to clichés, stereotypes, and stares
your Black peers impose. Pointed out
in their slideshows filled with Bible verses.
Always handy in their briefcases. Their bags.
Acting like your primary care physicians,
your spiritual advisors authorized to prescribe
daily doses of what is (and is not) *Good* for you.
Often without your permission,
Michael was one of those daily doses
many Black folks I knew wouldn't recommend.

Not then. Light-skinned,
saddled with bad acne every other week.
Some women may have called him *Cute*
on his good days, but they would have been
under the shade of the wrong tree.

For a time, we were casual friends.
He lived across the street.
Moved there after us,
he and his mom.
Didn't know her beyond snapshot motions.
I imagine she was afraid.

Mike was younger. Not my classmate.
We ended up walking down the same sidewalks
to the same bus stop on Lee Road.
Waiting for the 40 to go to the same suburb,
the same university.

We talked, not that much.
Long enough for me to hear him.
My first gay friend.
A lonely Black gay man.
I was certain. Certain he felt the laughter
when he wore his *Large Black Afro* wig to JCU.
Those exaggerated bell-bottom pants.
Platform shoes a clown might refuse.

Now, I sound like them, mocking him.
Mocking your peers,
just what young people do! Still do.
The only Black guy openly gay, wearing
huge fake hair in the suburbs.
How dare he!

He did not care.
Had no shame, even if they said he should.
Letting his emotions dictate his fashion choices,
not other people's fears.

Mike vanished one day.
Lingered long enough to say
he was moving to San Francisco.
That was before the 80s imploded,
all those flowers in people's hair.
Shrouded bodies after bodies after bodies,
grief covered cities like smog!
Where is My Michael now?

Black Sage at the Pulpit

You in College?

First in the Family?

You got Goals?

Cum Laude.   Magna Cum Laude   Summa Cum Laude.

What in the Lawde is Laude? Come on, somebody!

Black at a Black College?
Somewhere else **The Only One?**
Finish degrees quickly,
wherever you may be.
Wherever you may be! Come on, somebody!

GET SOME CHURCH UP IN HERE!
Praise teams, get up out of your seats.
Now You. Yes, YOU,
raise your Mortarboard,
toss it way up,
high up to the sky.
Kick your heels up.
Clap your hands. Bend down. Clap your hands.
Kiss the ground. Clap your hands.
Then sing YOU. Everyone to the heavens, SHOUT
THANK YOU!
THANK YOU!!!
Thank You, LAWD!!!
THANK   YOU,   LAWDE!!!
THANK   YOU,   LAWDEH!!!

THANK YOU!!!

THANK YOU!!!

THANK YOU!!!.

HIGH HEELS

"I couldn't wait until I grew up. I used to look at my mom's stockings and put them on with her high heels and mess with my hair."

—Florence Griffith Joyner

Shelving Our Library Books
Response poem to "The Closing" by Ravina Wadhwani

Put all the *Tressies*,
light-skinned with long, flowing hair,
straightened. *Wigs. Weaves.*
Black Beauties on front shelves.
Dark. Short Hair always near
restrooms or back-exit signs.

All the *Four Eyes. Braces?*
Put them in our big storage spaces
as soon as shipments arrive overnight.
First look at their copyright dates.
Check their spines.
Stamp their insides.
Immediately!

Exactly where do we put all those old novels?
Bony. Praying Mantis. Skinny Minnies.
Put them in the archives with
Waterhead. No-Ankles Ass.
Big-Lipped. Plain Old Ugly. Fatsos.
Always, always
next to *Angry*
and *Hair Kinky*.

Any questions?
Go to the Reference Desk.
Head Librarian will help.
A woman herself,
a wise enough expert
who claims to know where every
one of our books should go.

CFMP Part I

Teacher colleagues and I
used to wear high heels to work.
Shamelessly! At least three inches!
Some brave souls wore stilettos daily.
Imagine now, chasing an errant student
down the hall in those!

First-year rookie teacher, *Me*,
wore wedge boots once to school.
Better suited for Gene Simmons.
Made it that day.
Fashion's bold fool,
creeping across black ice and snow
in the parking lot.
More daring than a Wallenda
walking a long tightrope
across the Hoover Dam.
Other days, I wore platforms.
The weather up there was fine
most of the time.
Lost heels off my shoes? Yes!
Thank God, never while teaching.

High heels do not need
to be on the curriculum.
But we women teachers with style insisted.
A melting pot of us.

One Black math teacher
grew up with her mom training
her arches to accept
nothing less than elevation.
Great teacher! Great shoe attitude!
Her feet and legs learned early
never to tolerate flats.
FLATS, said like a four-letter word.
Never seen in schleppy sneakers
while on breaks or after school.
Probably under her desk or in her car?

Unseen. Soon forgotten.
She had her image down.

Dress for success. To impress.
High heels made us look
Professional
Respectable
Ladylike
Attractive
Empowered.
Whisper it: Sexy! Adults Only!

Nice heels hunger for dresses and skirts.
Any excuse to coordinate.
Have fashion fun on the job.
Matching dresses.
Matching shoes.
Matching purses.
Matching hats.
Matching tote bags.
Matching eyeshadow.
Matching lipstick.
Matching nail polish.
Matching pencils and papers.

Excess overboard?
Wear a leather or mink coat to teach.
At least one supervisor
came out to check on us
during winter, never without her obligatory
full-length mink coat.

Wearing it always reminded us to behave.
To stay several steps behind her designer heels.

CFMP Part II

Someone's wearing flashy high heels at work.
Someone must be having an affair.
Furtively following her lover's car after work.
Wearing Foster Grants when it's cloudy.
Not just women's feet flirting with foreign nations.
One or both married to the unsuspecting.
Want to know all the dirt?
Bring your lunch. Buy a Coke.
Lean back in the teachers' lounge.
Check papers on planning periods,
multitask while getting the play-by-plays
often told with stop-action videos.
Hotter than *Peyton Place* and
The Young and the Restless combined.
Some of the costars may make special
appearances before your next class.
Eyewitness *True Confessions* Live!

Your Two-Toned Shoes

White man, I should run.
Profile like a Rubens painting.
Boy band good-looking,
you make me want to stay.
Ready to deep-dive into all your Italian clichés.

Find out about your godfather.
Your soccer knees.
Why you love *Rocky*,
other Sly Stallone movies.
Rumors about your kisses.
Said to love Black women like De Niro.

Your crazy, curly hair like ours
that does twirls around your ears.
That goatee asking me
to look past stubble,
frown lines, and worried chins.

                    Can you?   Can I?
              Try something new for us in Cleveland?
Interracial dating?   Date a Black woman?
Date an Italian?

Ignore your hen-pecking mother.
                              Meddlesome office chatter.
The thoughts of people staring.
Glaring at us.
                Our eyes doing backflips
                    just for one another.

Put on my black platforms.
Put on your two-tone shoes.
    Yo, stepping out tonight.

                    Let's *fuggedaboutit*,
                    the rest of the world.

Do the Hustle!

Your red wrap dress.
Fiercest Black stilettos.
Girlfriends obstructing your targets.
He asked you to dance.

Let him lift you up on the
dance floor.
Still thin enough.
He dips you.
Hands clap.
You outdanced everyone.
Bubbles of gladness.
Coupling on dance floors
always allowed.

Fast music spinning.
DJ churns out a slow dance.
George Michael's "Careless Whisper."
Your jam.
Dance partner holds close.
Sometimes enough to allow
his attempts to start excavating.

You smile. Move his arms
carefully back up your spine.
Time for another fast number
to move his hands away
just in time.
"Disco Inferno." Ready to burn
all those female clocks in sight.

"Atomic Dog" gets everybody up,
whether coupled off
or gleefully dancing the night solo.

Shaking booties. Body parts forgotten.
Dance music and drinks reviving.

Bow-wow-wow, yippie-yo, yippie-yeah.
Bow-wow-wow, yippie-yo, yippie-yeah.

That night, you thought you met *HIM*.
Dogs must chase cats.
Do the dogcatcher, baby, do the dogcatcher.
Do the dogcatcher, baby, do the dogcatcher.
Your Hustle has just begun.

Reefer Madness

"I have never smoked reefer."
Gen Xers, their mommas and daddies —
they don't believe me.
Their eyes and laughter say,
"No way!"
Marijuana everywhere by the 60s.
The 70s. It's NEVER leaving the building —
or this planet.

Guys who liked me back in the day
had that catch phrase. An entry.
Never said any White Guy stuff like,
"Do you wanna come up and see my etchings?"
Brothers said,   "Do you wanna smoke some?"
                              Always blushed when I said, NO!
After disbelief started resting on their shoulders,
they usually disappeared into the
Darkness —
or I saw them propositioning someone else.

So many opportunities gone down toilets.
Many toilets. Some smoked at college dances. In clubs.
A little dancing.
A little drinky.   A little bud in the bathroom.
Probably just their booster shot, ready for something stronger.
In front of the mirror. Under the sink.
Inside a stall.   Open or closed.
Take a hit with friends or alone.
Dessert will be had after all.
The night was good.
Ain't goh' judge.

Got one better. Why not light up
in the movie theater?
The place coursing with beautiful folks.
Beautiful smoke. Almost made us choke,
Richard Pryor doing comedy on screen.

Sho' nuff he wouldn't have complained.
Not Cab Calloway or Snoop. Tell the truth,
reefer reeks worse than a skunk in heat.

Don't like reefer.   Don't like cigarettes.
Don't really drink.
Just holding a Rum and Coke as a prop,
giving off cool Approach-Me vibes.   Just wanting the old-timey stuff.
To be noticed.
In da club — any Buppie-approved club.
Some Brooks Brothers Brotha   sauntering my way.
Golden Fleeces are the best highs.

Pay Day

Before ATMs. Online banking. Direct pay.
Bank books, deposit slips, and bank tellers
were elevator music.
Always there, no matter what day or time.

Back then, Pay Days were like high school
graduations every other Friday.
My working family members and I always
headed for Key Bank on Chagrin Blvd.
Then Van Aken, we got into those ceremonial lines.
Sometimes standing long enough to have a
family or class reunion, depending upon how many tellers
were open and how fast the lines.

Ropes corralling us like horses
ready to run wild and free with some cash.
Excited with burning thoughts about
the moolah in our hands waiting to be spent.
Being in our twenties,
feeling like freshly pressed twenty-dollar bills,
the money flew out of our bank accounts
before birds could lightly feather new nests.

Buying what our eyes knew we could not afford,
new dresses and suits
at Kelly Kitt, May Company, and Higbee's.
Retail therapy to the max enhanced by credit.
If denied, another card, the understudy, was waiting.
Living beyond our means had no meaning.
Yes, we dressed for success, for church,
and for upwardly mobile boyfriends then.
To be seen by some *Black Young Urban Male Professional*

Aka Buppy. He might notice me
at our neighborhood club, The Forge,
the name sounded like a clone factory.
I look good, profiling in my matching
tan sweater, skirt set, and intelligent heels
waiting against the wall all by myself.

For a split second,
he might imagine seeing me
in his BMW.
He did finally
ask me to slow dance.
A future CPA driving a Camry.
Wedding poses over a decade later.

The Pugh Musketeers

After Big Sis rowed her boat
from our Talford home,
my two siblings and I were left.
Left to discover our own
transportation modes.
Got ideas from Mom's vociferous,
ceramic horse collection.

Valuing our freedom to roam,
we formed a new alliance.
We chose horses. Quarter Horses
we could ride together.
We began calling ourselves,
The Three.   The Three Musketeers.

Never assigning one another
specific character's names:
Not Athos, Porthos, or Aramis.
We never read those novels. All of us should have.
Not just me, the English Major. Mom always savored calling me that.
We eventually learned the author,
Alexandre Dumas was Black. Some say, Mixed-Race.
One quarter Black still means Black.
Did you know that? How about that?

What did we do after mounting our steeds?
Well, fully embracing foreign culture,
one of our favorite outings became
going to the cinema. Often to see subtitled movies.
Sounded more suitable for French guards
than just going to the movies to view box-office fluff.

Shaker Theatre. We walked there.
   Cedar-Lee. We road there.
      Center-Mayfield. We road there.
         The Cleveland International Film Festival. We road there.
            Downtown Hippodrome. We said, "Too far to walk or ride now."

TROIS. The Three Musketeers. Where else did we ride together? To restaurants, to clubs, and to concerts. Two different ones just for Bro. Jean-Luc Ponty. Also, Return to Forever. Premiere Jazz fusion mixologists. Stanley Clarke and Al DiMeola, bass and guitar. Piano maestro, Chick Corea. At the Agora, saw Al Jarreau just for me. Right On! Ride On!

    We Three. For years, we rode steeds together. Right On! Ride On!
    We Pugh Musketeers made hand-in-glove histories. We rode.
Following what should be
Every Black Family's Pledge. Motto. Every Family's Legacy:
"Tous pour un, un pour tous."   "All for one, and one for All."

No French Kisses

*"I have found men who didn't know how to kiss.
I've always found the time to teach them."*

—**Mae West**

His name was Jerry.
An Afro like one of the Jacksons.
Built like a wide receiver.
Came in wide for everything!
Light-Skin-Ded, meaning he was a
pleasing shade of vanilla ice cream,
clearly still Black inside.
What women called a *Fine Black Brotha*
with a Fine Job.
Pretty like Ali.
A guy we'd see on a
bachelor calendar. On the cover.

His name was Jerry.
An average name for what I thought
was an above-average catch of the day.
A guy I would *accidentally* spill my Rum and Coke on.
A ploy. For introductions at popular, upscale clubs.
Just a drop of my drink falling on
his outstretched, no-wedding-ring finger.
Not on his well-fitting suit coat.

His name was Jerry.
Living in Cleveland. Wall-to-wall vixens
grabbing golden tickets,
pushing me in front of the next semi-truck
or bus if needed.
Survivors of the game learn early.
Yes, bartering loge seats for ourselves.
With ease.

His name was Jerry.
Met him in church.
Ideal place, not always.

Prayers don't keep
his female stalkers away.
He was a true gentleman.
Held doors for me, even when
other men let them
drop back on me.
He never walked too far ahead.
Pulled out and pushed in chairs.
On cue. Just for me.

His name was Jerry.
So handsome. Such a gentleman.
Both young and attractive.
His looks made our movie a hit.
Folks rubbernecking us
everywhere we went.
Full-blown attraction.
Puzzle pieces getting lost.
Just won't fit.

Truth telling —
Jerry could not kiss!
Not even from a manual.
Not even if I read it slowly to him.
His delivery was so wet!
His tongue, so desperate.
Lion tamer, please help us.   Right now!

Lap dog! Slobber kisses!
Is this what almost drowning feels like?
A Swiffer Wet Jet across my lips?
Gasping for my life.
On the inside. Never outside.
Felt like rushing to clean myself each time.
Where's the nearest sink?
Acting tricks next to my lipstick.
He never suspected.

Great kisses are openers.
Romance's sustenance. Part of its mysteries.
Intimate gateways beyond enticing surfaces and veneers.
Beginnings! Alas, we ended
before starting the ultimate French Kiss.

No time to teach him.
Busy with needy students
who needed me more.
He never taught himself.

His name was Jerry.
No French Kisses!

Short Kings

I don't automatically look for tall men
cause many people consider me a *Jolly Green Female*.
It is mostly our long limbs and far reach giving that illusion.
If dating was an online store,
I would check the Tall box every time.
The *Taller*, the better.
Although eating proverbial soup off a Brotha's head is convenient.
Especially if there are no chairs
or the place is SRO.

So you wonder what I consider short?
This Sista is 5 feet 9 inches.
So anything South of that in a man is
Short!
Like cell phones, short men make this Honey have bad posture!
Neck muscle strain.
Even pain from peering down too much.
Like giraffes, we stilted people love looking up
at all the fine trees out there!
Craning my neck to look up at that catalog guy I once dated.
Never a problem.

Short is not derogatory.
No sir!
Runt. Midget. Tiny. Little Guy. Peewee. Napoleon!
Most men would not stand to be called any of those.
Especially by us.
Get it *Stand*?
I made a pun without trying.

Next question.
Have I ever dated short men?
Yes, not settling although sometimes it used to feel like it.
Being cute or
having a scintillating personality
automatically made him *Taller*.
Stacked heels help. One boyfriend all the time.
While I wore flats.
Then gravity was our friend.

And when we kissed, no one had to stand on a bench.
Or step stool.
I did not have to kneel.

So I guess my vertical adventures in dating have not been overly vertical
I mean standing up.
Not lying down.
I think more challenging mentally.

One of my little guys seemed to bring up the subject
of our height variations far more than I ever did.
Which tells us,
it bothered him more than a pimple on his face.
More than a receding hairline running last in a race.
Even if he knows he can do well in bed.

       So smallness in height men consider their Achilles heel?
   Kevin Hart has certainly made millions talking about vertical failings.
         Laughing with us all of the way to one of his mansions.
          God was the one, not I who made some men short.
   If I had superpowers, I would make every man at least 6 feet 2 inches.
             As tall as special Misters.
      Mr. Mamoa, Mr. Honsou, Mr. Snoop Dogg, Mr. Kodjoe.
             Even Mr. Silver Scott.
           Yes, the Tallest Property Brother.

Short Shorts

Hot Pants. Daisy Dukes. The names.
In my Cleveland and Indiana young, ready days,
there was a denim pair long gone.
My Italian almost-boyfriend said they looked good on me.
I wore them on purpose when he visited my home.
If not for the stretch marks,
I was beautifully bone-skinny.

Wore short shorts out in public,
no outcries.
Not even from my parents,
who always scrutinized.
Back in the 70s, miniskirts were fine.
Wore a minidress when I graduated college.
Our clothing choices then had nothing to do
with decency or our book knowledge.
So one could say that was the time
women were allowed to be brazenly undressed in tube tops, no bras,
such and such, without being called a you-know-what!

An important caveat. Men sometimes catcalled me.
A word I learned as an adult when they were no longer calling.
But back in the day, they called me "Slim."
"Hey, Slim. Heyyyyyyyyyyy, Slim!"
Ain't gon' lie. I was very young. Liked being noticed by strangers.
Did not realize what catcalling really means.
These were young men cruising around in cars
looking for trouble — or to make some.
Back then, the calling out was seemingly innocent.
Yet somehow empowering to them and to me.
But slowing gas pedals with idling engines were not.

Was never accosted in short shorts.
Made sure when one older man slowly followed me and my shorts,
in his old, rumbling car.
That was near Purdue University, when I was in grad school,
just walking in my khaki, *let's take a stroll* pair.

Times changed rapidly.
Some men got bolder.
Snatching fully-clothed women
out of their heels in broad daylight.
Almost happened to me,
walking through Tower City.
Minding my feet and business in my 30s.
Thank God, for 20/20 in the back of my head,
saw a would-be, could-have-been,
never-was-assailant following me. Thank God for security.

Cleveland Metroparks Love

Lovemaking in a public place.
Perfect picnic ending.
I was willing. You were not.
No fear of ants enjoying us.
Spread out our bright, plaid blanket.
Nature will never judge us.

Under the stars, illuminating foreplay.
I unzip you as your tender voice
massages my neck first,
then the air all around us.

Coyotes croon as we moan/spoon
under the blood moon.
We are banging.
Banging! Banging!
No apartment neighbors
wall banging, making us stop.

Our skin is open.
Fingertips/lips open.
A mad symphony so joyous.
No scolding chorus.

                Just Love as it should be.
                Finally a-LOUD!

Stereophonic echoes into the night.
Let's stay here until park rangers'
flashlights chase us home.

Let's try love in the rain next time.

                All these fantasies you never allowed.

B-I-T-C-H

A word women know intimately.
Better than any ex or potential lover.
Only been called **B-I-T-C-H** a few times
by men. Well, one a mere boy.
All meant to topple me in my stilettos.
Riding like a gladiator into my own arenas,
someone always there throwing spears
and spikes to disable my chariots.
My beautiful, black horses.

Women still attempting to burn bras.
Longing for freedom trash cans.
Ready to stop dreaming about knights.
Or would-be knights.
No longer caring about accouterments.
Not worrying about any civility.
Profanity now officially America's comfort food.

He swore at me. Not me at him.
Hope kept me cordial.
My Black boyfriend, later husband,
calling my bluff. Then calling not my name,
but those dreadful five letters!
Both of us prime, not even 30.
Breaking up barely. Plan B hatched
cause he couldn't "Put a Ring on It."

Thank you, Beyoncé, for that song,
which came out much later.
Back then, we had Aretha's "Respect,"
Helen Reddy's "I am Woman,"
Chaka Khan's "I'm Every Woman,"
Gloria Gaynor's "I Will Survive."
Those anthems on our crests and shields.
Finally thrusting our chests for ourselves.

Tired of waiting for bended knees
and Cinderella-slipper fittings.
My story needed to finally be about ME!
This **B-I-T-C-H** shrugged for several minutes.
Blazed into grad school
on a scholarship magic carpet.
God help me, kept envisioning
his bended knee and future babies.

Grad School Blues

My landline had a thyroid problem.
Sometimes the calls came in quicker
than rabid fans calling rock stars' private numbers.
Always at the most inconvenient times!

Family often synonymous with *Co-dependency*.
Calling to find out if I still love them.
Are they kidding?
Deadlines up my ass while
family continues to need validations!
Or was it something else?
Their need to still control the buttons
all the way from Cleveland?

If I don't answer, can't they figure out I'm
talking to Shakespeare or Aristotle or Ong?
Smoke signals to my family won't do.
Yet whatever one of them wanted was always
more important than finishing my paper after paper
after paper due the next day.
Or grading student papers after student papers
after student papers. Attach the required rubrics.
Or prepare my next English 101 lesson plans.
Don't forget required office hours every week!

So after my family members kept calling,
taking turns like hamsters on treadmills,
I couldn't ignore their phone calls anymore.
Which usually amounted to chit chat ending
with a random selection from our *I Love Lucy* playlist.

If they really loved me, they would have given me space
to type, a *Do or Die* grad school paper
which often drove me to the typing room late at night.
To use an electric typewriter I couldn't afford to own.
Walking across a slasher-movie threshold late at night.
All by myself. With Pepsi liquid courage
to help keep me awake. Alert.

No *Norman Bates*.
No *Chucky* jumping out from the shadows.

Some evenings chucking it all,
I went into Young Grad Hall's television room
to relive *Who Shot J.R.?*
I was rarely alone.

Here Comes the Bride!

Are we blessed?
Or forever dodging curses?
Has anyone ever lived a fairy tale?
Did Princess Di?
Does anyone?
Not even on the covers of *Ebony*, *Jet*,
or *People* magazines?

Late on my own wedding day.
Rain on my own wedding day.
Hard luck trains seem to follow me.
Basking in bliss and budgets,
making sure laughter still prevails.

Family and friends waiting at the church.
Wondering if I'm a runaway bride.
My fiancé pretending his black suit was confident.
His best man spoon-feeding him affirmations.
Love still prevailed so…

He waited.
They waited.
Everyone waited.
Late at least thirty minutes?

Why the delay?
Took too many perfectionist pills that day?
Voices telling me living at home is still okay?
Louder inner voices saying,
"Still living at home, single at 34. Not okay."

No glam squads at my disposal
unless playing most of the lead roles counts.
Nail tech, always miscast.
Should have worn white gloves.
Did not think of that.
Except for my butchered tips,
I was fit for the top of any wedding cake.

Then unlacing that wedding train, so I can go to the bathroom.
A designer's sick joke.
More like a straitjacket with too many ties.
My sister Michelle, maid of honor, mastered it in one day.
Who knew marriage would be far more complicated?

The night before, my brain was befuddled.
Wrapping bird seeds in mesh with ribbons.
So pretty and delicate!
So proud I had done it all myself.
To this day, I do not know who stole my creations!
Stole them inside the church!
Someone who enjoyed seeing me sabotaged.
So, no shower of eco-friendly well-wishes for us as we drove away.

No memorable photos, because the photographer
turned out to be insanely unprofessional.
What professional doesn't know how to prep his own equipment?
Grateful we had a few borrowed photos.
Saved some wedding cake for a year.
And a save-the-day video that still makes me laugh
and cry.

Flowers

Her always-soft, loving grasp gave me
wildflowers that day —
an offering to me.
She insisted warmly,
"Place them in water immediately!"
I only protested for a minute.
How could I refuse my mother, who always knew?
Mom always knew more about taking care of flowers than I did.
Knew more about poetry
and so many other things before we did.

When I married, moved away, she gave me
her wedding portrait with Daddy,
blessing and watching over my apartment. *Me*.
Where all my visitors could see their faces.
Eager love, ready for new flavors.
Mom always said that Dad called her
"Dynamite" when they first met.
Destined. Had to marry.

It was an easy home wedding where
Daddy bought layered cake needing icing
while Mom made her own bouquet.
Roses, gladiolas, ferns supported by a coat hanger.
That's what she told me proudly.
They always liked getting things done themselves.

Mom and Daddy planted again in spring without our help.
More annuals, easy to maintain.
Red and pink roses eventually framing our home.
Lawn my mother sometimes mowed herself.
Mom and Dad were like those rose bushes.
Arriving every year when we needed to see them the most.
I loved their beauty.

Their embraces never impeded by thorns.
Their leaves dancing so close,
always intertwining for strength around us.

Tethered

for Marvin, my husband

In bed, I loved our tethers.
Your Mister Magic sax voice first tied us together.
Ravished by whispers.
Silent and succulent kisses.
Conjoined connections, again and again.
Wishing to keep tricking dreaded absolutes and nevers.
Sinking us into and above. Beyond.
Believing our lovemaking
defined how *Immortals* lived and loved.

Listening to our buoyant body sounds forever,
forgetting the white, plastic blinders and blunders in our lives.
Losing our breaths in insensitive air always filling
that annoying burgundy-red Dodge
perpetually driving us into crazy somewhere.
Places we could never go together. Only in bed.
Places we despised alone. When anger,
sometimes rage, lead us out of our true homes.

Satin on necks now. Hands. Legs. Feet.
Opulence and newness. Everywhere!
Gently pulling us in.
Succumbing to all flavors. All mutual commands.
Sweet scents of my Calvin Klein and your Paco Rabanne.
Pillows holding our joy again and again.
Those memories tether us forever.

Our love is Sade strong.
We gotta hang on.
We gotta hold on.
We gotta hang on.
We gotta hold on.
Hang on, Love.
Hold on. Hold on.

Our Giant Steps
for Marvin

Sonny Fortune played "Song for My Lady"

  another NOJS concert date night. So vivid.

    We strolled through weekends

      taking us where we wanted

        and needed to go. Ordered another

          vegetarian pizza.

            Drank bottles of Schlitz or Heineken.

            Drank in all the liquid affirmations

              from White and Black couples

                who said we look good holding hands

                walking down Coventry Road,

                down any road together.

                  Always hearing our jazz better like that.

                  Or underneath fireworks after Indians

                    games. Lighting fires for dream homes and babies.

                    Big plans are happy cornets like Nat Adderley's.

                      Or luscious   saxophones   like Coltrane's.

Two-Paycheck Plan

CP time does not define us.

Black couples should hold hands on escalators.
                  Two paychecks require boxing gloves.
Sparring.   Mainly with *Them*.   Punch time clocks.

                  Not each other!

Why do some husbands make wives wait for too many things?
        It took *You* NINE years before deciding to finally marry *Me*!
Two paychecks.
Always the plan.
Shared bill payments.
Shared saving accounts.
Stick to the plan. Not the pain. Withdrawing money without real conversations!
                  Strike One!
Some marathon spring mornings were savored and sweet.
              Not those making *Me* late again. For work.
You spent weeks in the bathroom.
Shaving while debating with Perfection and Happiness.
Leaving Me about a second
in the shower to Procrastinate.
Then hopping into my clothes,
Then inside our gassed-up coffin just for two.
                  Strikes Two, Three, and Four!
Where *You* chose not to speak
while I tried forming words more concrete.
Explaining to *The Boss*
why I was late again.
Arriving hearing that familiar sternness.
           "Mrs. Hamer, your pay may be docked soon."
                  Strike FIVE!
Buying my own car. *I* told *You*,
even though you threatened

to leave me if *I did*.
Sometimes risks must be taken.
              I Did!
Ding. Ding. Ding!!!   **Teddy's LOVE TKO?**

Sometimes changes shake their heads. Sometimes eventually has her sway.
More idle, big voice threats
Your tired back away from *Mine*.
Finally letting go inside one another. Pillow talking again.
Splashing Pendergrass kisses all over lips and limbs.
Lose plans. Make new ones.
Always put more **L-O-V-E** inside banks.
Inside our joined hands and plans.

High Heels

A young male clerk joked yesterday about
women of certain ages resigning themselves.
Listen to flat shoes.
Buy them.
Nurse them.
Comfortable Naturalizers are souls
strolling in rose gardens.

But Tina Turner says,
"Burn those ugly shoes!
Go to Nordstrom.
Buy black stilettos, red slingbacks,
turquoise platforms that giggle.
Speak our name and his.
Shout without permission.
Shoes that are always seen.
Even in closets.

Women must never forget their high standards —
Manolos, Louboutins, Jimmy Choos,
Knockoffs, Nine Wests from Marshall's.
All the time.
Any time!
Feet, even old feet,
put on real women's shoes!

Toes no longer twenty,
possibly bent,
can still get high when women
admire themselves in mirrors.
Legs looking long, long, longer, and LONGER!

Let leather tickle us head to toe like Tina!
Prance. Do the Pony, girl!
Become windmills who never hesitate.
Whirling, twirling, without tilting or falling.

Free.
Finally.
Free to strut down our runways all the time!

FLAT SHOES

"I can't wear flat shoes. My feet repel them. I was in agony. My high heels had left my feet bleeding. Laugh all you want, my feet hurt."

—Mariah Carey

Teacher Assault Boot Camp Training

Level One:
The Dress and The Drills

Teachers, always come dressed in your appropriate urban public school tactical gear. Only the standard-issue garments. The kind that mercenaries put on like underwear. This clothing will soon feel like your second skin. Daily dress checks, mandatory. You may be punished or sent home if you wear shorts. If you don't pass inspections, you'll be assigned extra duties. Hall monitoring or recess. Replacement attire is always available for discount at all our approved barracks outlets.

Memorize! Drill into your heads daily! Stop Believing All of the Following:
Holding hands and singing songs is forever.
Your gentle voice will change everything.
You will always sleep at least eight hours,
even though you must plan lessons and check papers
into the wee hours. Evenings. Mornings. Weekends.
You will never have to repeat (repeat) yourself.
All kids like to be told what to do.
All kids look up to you.
All students will love walking single-file
cause it's easier than writing cursive.

All kids love the grades you give them,
so parents and principals will never ask you to change any.
Cause student athletes and seniors never fail!
Paper airplanes, broken pencils, aging paperbacks, and eager spitballs.
None of those will ever fly past you like in a tornado.
No one will ever purposely stick gum on the seat of your favorite work chair.
No student will ever remove your borders
or completely destroy your inspiring bulletin boards.

No student will ever spit into your coffee! Or spit on you!
No students will ever fistfight. You will never have to break one up.
No parent will ever verbally or physically threaten you.
No active shooter will ever skulk near classrooms
while everyone hides behind desks and shadows.
No one in schools will ever suffer.
No one will ever develop PTSD —
that's only for soldiers in the military.

Memorize these, too:
Drink barrels of caffeine.
Dive into Bayer aspirin baths.
Sneak vodka during lunch time.
See shrinks to shrink your dreams.

Memorize the Do Not List:
Do not use up your sick days.
Do not get wounded.
Do not have heart attacks.
Do not die in the line of duty.
Do not carry guns. Not yet!

Level Two:
Read Our Active-Duty School Archives—
The Middle School Desk

The Middle School Desk.
                      Young girl careened into the classroom
at the sound of the bell. We always tell the never-listening not to run
into danger.
                    The heavy desk she bumped into was a grenade that landed
                            on top of her teacher's right foot. Accident or not,
the pain and swelling both ached to be barefoot in sand all the time.
                Even while working. Even while sleeping.

Level Three:
Read Our Active-Duty School, Police & Juvenile Court Archives—
The High School Door

The High School Door.
                Who is that teenage boy running down the hall?
                    Why is that middle-aged, female teacher chasing him?
                        Pursuing him with hounds as far as she could,
he disappeared into the anonymity of usual.
Late students **BLAMming** lockers. Closed doors
with no surprises behind them.
Why? Female Teacher was standing ushering students
inside as the warning bell rang. Closing her door.
Almost.

Halfway inside another sardine can of noise
that typically comes before silence.
                        Right then, he slammed her door harder than hard
                           against the backboard of her lower back.
                        Attempting to shatter it!
                                Releasing torpedoes of intense PAIN.
                    "PLEASE, addict her to painkillers, PAIN!"
That was no accident!
The school refused to report the incident.
Never thoughts of AWOL,
protecting her troops of one,
Female Teacher had to break rank.
Went to the local police that day
on her way home
before wisely calling in sick for a few.
Before the hearing got scheduled.
Before going back into combat.

                    Hazard pay. Workman's Comp.
                    That money never mattered.
          "Give us back our dignity, or give us death!"

                        The whistle blows.
        "Get back into teacher formation. Ten-hut!"

                            "Yes, sir!"

School Fashion Police

Part One

Wrong choices make you
feel like putting a bag over your head
when you walk to your next class
wearing that same top you wore last week!
Or wearing that same top two days in a row
because you did not go home.
Do you and your family members believe in clean clothes?

Someone always knows.
Might as well announce it on the PA.
If someone would act as your seeing
eye dog, you would welcome
them as your guide, avoiding the embarrassment of not
dressing up-to-date like *that crowd*.

There is always *that crowd* and *that kid*
who loves being a trendsetter,
even when other kids snicker.
They rarely follow his lead.
The fake *trendsetters* seem to have outfits
for every day of the week in more colors
than Baskin-Robbins has flavors.
One popular student rumored
to be a drug dealer could somehow always
afford matching outfits — head to fancy kicks.

While others are relegated
to wearing *buddies* with
hand-me-downs because some
are homeless, trying their
best to be fashion-ins.
Denying they are fashion-outs
living in shelters or group homes.

Part Two

I remember that White boy with the cool
mohawk porcupine quills.
Made most of the kids
laugh in front of his back, especially after
they looked down at his tight, tight
jeans screaming to be released
from his oblivious, scrawny butt.
So, kids laughed. Laughed
him out of our school.
One day. Just one
day, he was their classmate.
One day. Never saw him again.
Guess he went looking for his
fashion amigos?
Or became another ninth-grade dropout?

Part Three

Before Eric Clapton "Shot the Sheriff,"
Black students frequented barbershops
where they got fades along with the latest gossip.

At our school assembly,
they prepped to zap our guest speaker
for wearing *dreadlocks*
because clearly he was not one of us.
A Martian ready to harm us?

Black students not knowing.
Not knowing.
Not knowing Marley would
one day mesmerize.
Wake masses from false trances.
Sing songs filled with hyacinth splendor.
Save many from carrion slumber.
Save many modern-day slaves like us.

Teenage Suicide Poem

They glisten in the imagination.
Flesh and metal conjoining to release agony.
Huffing or cutting mere hobbies.
The allure of ropes, razors, knives, and pills.
Monoxide filling nostrils.
Spoilers will discover you too soon.
A 9 mm, the quick comforter for soldiers
that captures the moment. Click!

Better than any Nikon SLR camera. Click!

Captures minds wishing for solace.
That freedom to a heaven forbidden.
A respite from wars.
Not really. Probably a flight to them.
An inferno of nothingness.
A freedom from the weights
of *Earthliness* nonetheless.

Click!

Click!

Click!

Cleveland on Fire

I.

Cleveland, famous for headlines
catching on fire like our Cuyahoga River.
Water ablaze happened at least a dozen times.
Filled with oil slicks
and dead rats almost as big as dogs.
No one cared until 1969.

II.

Cleveland, a place where some monster
held three women captive.
Forcing them to live
in boarded up squalor and fear.
On the West side.
Students of mine knew one of the victims.
Three raped and abused for ten years!
There is a special place in hell for men who
make girls become mothers
before they can learn to love their own bodies.

A Black knight saved all of them.
Brought a disjointed Hollywood happy ending.
Their escape led to a trial.
Finally incarcerated, crazed men find religion?
Become repentant.
Or commit suicide.

III.

    Cleveland, also the place where they said they captured
        a Nazi war criminal.
    Said he was Ivan the Terrible. Of course, **DE NIAL**
        was John Demjanjuk's river.
The Feds sent him to Israel to pay for his sins. Tried more than once.
        There is no **DE NYING!**
Men, women, and children were taken, tortured, and killed.
        All disposed of like landfill.
    Consciences still burn in bonfires for eternity.
    John Demjanjuk might not have been him.
        No DE NYING!
Ivan the Terrible should have died over and over again.

HAVE YOU SEEN HER?

NAME: XXXX X XXXXXX   **AGE:** 16
HEIGHT: 5 feet   **HAIR:** Black
WEIGHT: 140 Lbs.   **EYES:** Brown

ATTIRE: Blue and white Dodger Starter Jacket, white Kent State University T-Shirt in blue lettering, blue jeans with a black belt, brown deck shoes, and gold triangular earrings.

LAST SEEN: Saturday, XXXXX XX, 19XX, 11 a.m. in the vicinity of XXXXXX XXXXXXXXXXXXXXXXXXXXXXXXXXXXXXXXXXXXXXXX

IF YOU HAVE INFORMATION, PLEASE CONTACT THE CLEVELAND POLICE DEPARTMENT AT XXX-XXXX or XXX-XXXX.

REWARD OFFERED!

CLEVELAND HEADLINES, WE WILL NEVER FORGET!
SWEET, YOUNG, BLACK GIRL!

She was *That Black Girl!* **ANOTHER YOUNG, GIFTED,** and **BLACK GIRL!** Megawatt smile illuminating beauty, intelligence, promise, and God's grace. Quick-thinking enough to win any marathon race. Some people just make everyone want to finish what they started. **SWEET, YOUNG, BLACK GIRL!** Never bought that prom dress. Never wore our white cap and gown. Never finished high school. **MISSED** her entire senior year!

I only knew her in passing, but still say I knew her. Passed her in the hallways before classes. Recall saying "Hello" because she was someone who never feared being friendly or kind. Was she an angel sent to teach us? She helped make morning announcements over the PA. Like morning coffee there to awaken and ease everyone's day. Her voice. Her face. Everything about her was RIZZ. Seemed like a poster girl for **HAPPINESS** and **CONFIDENCE**. Imagining **Daughter** or **Friend** embroidered inside her jackets. **YOUNG, GIFTED, AND BLACK GIRL! ALL TEACHERS and PEERS. OUR SCHOOL KNEW HER. ADMIRATION WALKED BESIDE HER. WE WILL NEVER FORGET HER!**

Enough to already be deeply saddened and horrified,
even before they found
HHHHHH---EEEEEE---RRRRRRRR! SWEET, YOUNG, BLACK GIRL.

When I came back from miscarriage sick leave, my students, **MANY** told me, **"SHE'S MISSING!" MISSING for SEVERAL DAYS** that turned into **WEEKS! MONTHS! WE LOST COUNT. FORGOT HOW TO COUNT. STOPPED COUNTING! POSTED COUNTLESS FLYERS** covered with **COUNTLESS TEARS**. Looked throughout our **COUNTLESS COMMUNITIES** for **SWEET, YOUNG, BLACK GIRL.** Flashlights flooded streets and fears. Every shrieking unintelligible sound shouted. Can you hear? Can you see?

HAVE YOU SEEN HER?

Then **ONE DAY KNEW**. Rancid smells in a neighborhood backyard told, **EVERYONE, STOP!** We were freeze-framed at that moment. Like figures in a wax museum. Like participants in some psychopath's sick human chess game. **A mistake?** Some wanted to continue looking corner to corner even then. LOOKING for **SWEET, YOUNG, BLACK GIRL! PLEASE, STOP LOOKING!**

The search for her **KILLER** didn't take **MONTHS or WEEKS. MERE DAYS!** A **BLACK GIRL** whose **BLACK BOYFRIEND** allegedly killed her. Soon pronounced **GUILTY!** Alleged he butchered her! Worse than a thousand deaths to someone already dead. In court, he claimed he never treated her body like a cutlet. A large, serrated knife. His fingerprints still kissed it. That merciless baseball bat. They argued. He claimed he might have made her fall to the kitchen floor. She never got up anymore. Then, in court, he pleaded the incisions were not his. Claiming someone else's cruel hands permanently hushed her.

That heinous hacksaw. Desperation. Depravity. Humanity brutally dismembered. Then discarded. Disposed of in bags made for garbage. Decomposition disrespected even her good heart. Never found her complete body parts! Bleach can never wash away our many blood-stained thoughts. Still embedded inside. Still tearing minds apart. Can you see? Can you hear that sickening sound? That terrifying feeling of being lost and really never found?

BLACK GIRL MAGIC
FFFFFRACTURED FFFFFOOOOEEEEEVVVVVEEEEERRRRR!

WE ALL STILL MOURN!   **SWEET, YOUNG, BLACK GIRL!**
MISSED FOREVER!
ANOTHER YOUNG, GIFTED, and BLACK GIRL never coming back home.

STILL PRAYING for THE MISSING.
PLEASE.   *PLEASE COME BACK!*
SWEET, YOUNG, GIFTED, AND BLACK GIRLS!

TODAY, **ANOTHER** AND **ANOTHER** AND **ANOTHER STOLEN**.
STILL MISSING,
OVER 97,000 LAST YEAR. STILL COUNTING. STILL COUNTING
BLACK GIRLS AND **BLACK WOMEN. MISSING!**

HAVE YOU SEEN THEM???

HAVE YOU SEEN US???

BULLY

Another heart-stopping
crowd of carnivores in a school.
One voracious reptile unleashed,
a python snapping its mouth
to attention for its feast.
Reeling another head from side to side.
Releasing venom quickly.
Tasting blood.
More blood seeking another victory
in a classroom, spilling into hallways,
convulsing involuntarily,
attempting to ingest all of that taste,
that taste of pride remaining on the floor.
Trapped prey smaller, but unafraid,
struggling against such force.
Still fighting. Fighting.

As few, including this teacher,
tried to stop the words —
now fists while most just watch.
Some placing mental bets or real ones.
Waiting for their share,
cowering in conspicuous corners
with shadows made by cowards,
never emerging. Never helping.
Rushing forth last minute just to see,
then reluctantly away as
security decided this time, too late.

Another uneven fight is over.
But this time, the
Bully finally lost.

Bus 39 in America

Young Black wives wonder, "Why do banshees careen around our corners so early? Are dreams nightmare realities we refuse to believe?"

Bus 37, 1963 came for Medgar Evers.
The bus driver ghost said, "You already know. Rosa Parks and 1956 mean nothing here. Only window-dressing there. Go sit in the back where you will always belong."

Bus 39, 1965 came for Malcolm X.
The bus driver ghost said, "Heard you went to Mecca last year. What took you so long? Yes, go sit in the back where you belong."

Bus 39, 1968 came for Dr. Martin.
"The bus driver ghost said, "Your 'I Have a Dream' speech and demonstrations mean nothing here. No special seat for Peace up front. You still have to sit in the back where you belong. Be quiet!"

That same Bus 39 came years later, 1992, for Marvin Hamer.
The bus driver ghost had to speak louder, "After all these years, sitting in offices with White folks and your fancy college degrees, you still must sit in the back. I said you belong there. So go on. Sit down, fast!"

My beloved husband.
County Coroner said,
"Died of natural causes. Died of a coma."
No gun blasts. No headlines. No investigations.
To the coroner, Marvin was
merely another morbidity stat.
Another young Black man
dead in America consigned to keep
riding a bus designed
to have no clear destination, except death.
Not enough cheerful begonia "to or from" points on the maps.

My GE alarm buzzing, I reach for air. So thankful I was asleep. Now awake. So thankful there is no ghost driver intruder. My dream weaver had played a horrible trick on me again. Relieved that the ghost driver, only a figment of my imagination, determined to menace My Slumber. My Grief. My Life.

"Please, God, grant our Black men some peace.
Now and in heaven. Please grant Black women some too. Amen."

Spring Cleaning

In bitter January, when Cleveland ice
and snow chased all of us inside
to warm and thaw together in our beds,
you died sleeping alone in ours.
I had to isolate for impending surgery.
Checked on you at intervals.
We both thought it was "only the flu."
Tried to revive you.
Diabetes took you anyway.

I tried removing your scent from everything.
Removing your tax papers. Your *Wall Streets*.
Your *Black Enterprises!* Stacks. Stacks
you loved keeping like keepsakes.
Loved reading.
Reading about any
and everybody's business for breakfast.
while neglecting taking care of ours.

So much cleaning left for my hands.
Spring Cleaning.
Cleansing for days. For weeks. For years.
Breaking skin on fingers to fill that addictive need.
Clorox Bleach and praying on scarred knees.

Making bold moves.
Throwing away the covers
where we would never make love again
after watching *60 Minutes*.
Where you would never hold my back again.
Buying white, low-count bedsheets for new memories.
Stripping our queen bed of all our sad things,
yet somehow keeping the threads of happiness.
Happiness when we held hands anywhere.
Happiness widows must learn to grab for themselves.
Now, my hands forced to buy a new mattress alone.
Give away most of your business suits.
Other clothes sold at consignment.
Keeping your wing-tipped shoes.

Keeping your crisp, white handkerchiefs,
at least for a year, until they start to fray my nerves.
Keeping your brown, leather briefcase and awards.
We must remember you were here.

Thanking God and best man Glenn who
took all your accounting books away.
They could no longer stay as guests in the guest room.
Please take them from that room I always hated
where you boxed all your secrets
that almost died with you.
Where you made secret calls to her.
Kept notes and cards confirming you cheated.
Whispers lingering in our apartment
where I chose to live,
to sleep another 17 years!

Our last home together.
A two-bedroom apartment.
Never made it to our house.
Apart for too long.
Oddly safe inside that bedroom inside my head.
Always inside my heart.

Your scent taught me to love.
Also to distrust. **Monogamy**. **Marriage**. **Most Men**.
So for now, I keep cleaning.

Chagrin Boulevard

Finding your grave is a hopscotch game.
That oak tree on the left guides me to your willow tree.
That Jewish man nicknamed "Rabbi" always beside you.
He died young — like you, my love.
The untended ground around you is so dry and barren.
Very little grass with a few weeds determined to disturb your slumber.

A slight film of mud and dust now camouflages
your Cathedral Red Granite gravestone I chose.
"Beloved husband, son, brother." Your name. Dates.
All in black Roman letters. The Black is fitting.
Also, the letters, because you took Latin in high school.
You used to tell me, "Amo te." Not "Te amo."

I did bring flowers a few times. You need something permanent.
Like a fence with white pebbles dancing inside.
I should at least wash surfaces down before snow comes.
I do have a little first aid kit in my car.
Just for you and me, my beloved late husband.

I remember wishing our space was quieter.
The willow tree's breezes always soothed me.
Not that constant blare from cars passing on Chagrin Boulevard —
the actual name of the street. It needs a new one.

At least sometimes, we were alone for a change.
No Memorial Day swarms of sad people driving tearful cars.
At least one time, true freedom communed with us.
For almost thirty peaceful minutes.
I once said, "I'm painting my Cavalier a lively Mediterranean Blue."
You were elated that I still appreciated bright colors without you.

At the end of our visits, remember our rituals?
I would fold my hands. Recite "The Lord's Prayer."
Lay both palms down on our gravestone.
Make the sign of the cross. Just like the one in stone.
Psalm 46:11, "Lord is our refuge" always greeted us when
I visited our grave at least ten times. Many more just in our minds.
That last talk under our willow tree, I knew. We both knew
I had to let go of your arms. I reached until you finally released me.

Murray Hill

Breathe.
Years ago, three days after Halloween,
sped through Little Italy.
Ended up on one of their main streets
after making a wrong turn.
Was it the spirits
or curiosity that drove my blue car there that evening?

Breathe.
Up Murray Hill,
where angry men with aquiline noses,
descendants of Hannibal,
some of them as dark as me,
who used to yell and throw rocks
at colored folks' cars invading their sacred zones.

Breathe.
Was more like the West where some of us live now.
Remember Parma?
Where rednecks used to paint "NIGGERZ" on garages.
In their favorite color, RED!
Hung effigies in oak trees,
Or staked crosses in lawns.
The KKK wanted to have a parade
through downtown Cleveland once.
Never happened? Don't think so.

Breathe.
This Little Italy of long ago.
Generally peaceful, as long as everybody looked like them.
Nothing like Boston or New York though, much smaller.
Still known for those big, intermittent scary sounds,
That's what I read. And what my Daddy said.

Breathe.
He used to say "Never drive through there!"
He had many times.
One of his shortcuts home.
Because he was from Tuskegee, Alabama,
never afraid of anything.

Breathe.
Not even when alone.
He continued his sermon to me,
"You will not like what you see on their faces
or hear coming out of their throats.
We are not welcome, not even
at their famous Feast of Assumption parades!"

Breathe.
Mixed with defiance,
believing in fall signs,
felt safe to drive up that hill for the first time.

Breathe.
Aromas of basil and oregano from Margarita's restaurant
would one day welcome me.
Others like me would walk down those streets.
Then linger to eat smoked salmon pizza and calamari.
Never tasted calamari before in the evening.

Breathe.
But this time, long ago, I only
looked from my driver's seat. Did not linger.
Drove to the other side, felt like a thousand universes away.
To enter my sacred Eastern suburbs, integrated, filled with my people!

Breathe.
I drove up Mayfield quicker than Jesse Owens ran in Berlin,
capturing another gold medal for agility and courage.
Just me, steering that little blue Chevy,
propelling me toward zones that were safer back then.
Cleveland Heights. Then Shaker Heights home.

B-R-E-A-T-H-E.

Goin' Fishin'
for Daddy

Daddy had made me a promise
that he and I would go fishin'.
A lazy day to skip stones. Share stories
broader than biplane wings.
Would never be boring.
Just father with youngest daughter.
Leaving Mom and Micki at home.
Sounded easy. Nothing ever easy.
Hard removing stitches from family
when the knit loops so tightly.

He always called me *Patsy*.
No one else ever did.
Banana bunches, special delivery
just for me.
Feeling special in a family of six,
he made easy.
Returning the favor,
bought him a fishing rod.
A kit. Even a canvas vest.
One with a million pockets
for lures and things
he might have one day explained to me.

Grown city gal deprived of summers
on Lake Erie or one of its tributaries.
No sitting on eager cabin porches with him
spinning tales about big marlins.
No swatting mosquitoes in
Steinbeck or Sounder country.
Just stale air and steam heat
radiating from uneven Cleveland streets.
Me. Still missing always-warm places
where only we two could have gone together.
Sullen Childhood Me! Only sometimes.
Mom rescued. Did teach me
somethin' about fishin'!
Mainly in her kitchen.

I ate up delicious tutelages regarding
codfish, catfish. Even swordfish.
Spent hours studying fishin' for men.
Continued to need more of those lessons.

Daddy's fishin' remained on many terrains,
but never as a father on water
where we both belonged.
Sad and funny,
Dad had a fishing license, never used.
Found years later in his commode
right next to tons of old lottery tickets.

Never laying blame in his living room.
Sometimes, routines replace merry dreams.
I know he wanted to go fishin'.
Loving his apology hugs. Never needed.

The boat he rowed most of his life was life.
Up and down streams.
Destination always home. Family.
An aging wife. Another daughter.
Both needing him more,
waiting on his shore.
Waiting.

Red
for Mommy

Her color was *Red* for certain things.
Not everything!
Not because it was her favorite. *Green* was her favorite.
Not because we buried her in a *Red* dress
wearing one of her favorite *Navy* church hats.
Not because it was her chosen shade of lipstick.
Not because she painted her fingernails that color.
She was *Woman*, but rarely wore nail polish.
Her three daughters were just like her in that respect.

Her color was *Red*.
Not because she loved to see things and people bleed.
Never insisted on matching tees or outfits in *Red*.
Never bought an SUV in *Crimson Red*.
Never had those kinds of desperate needs.

Her color was *Red* because she could *Read*.
Read books and magazines. More importantly
could *Read* our faces. Trying to fulfill
her husband and children's every need.
She always gave us the bandages first.

As for her, she needed *Red* roses.
Red American beauties.
No other color.
And she insisted on writing her checks out in
unforgettable *Red* ink.
In curlicue cursive handwriting I always loved.
Red was my mother's color then!

Mom had a fortress of BIC pens with *Red Ink*.
Dad worked, sometimes two jobs,
while Mom paid all of our bills in *Red Ink!*
Sometimes right before seeing the proverbial *Red!*
My parents both died in 2005.
Mom first. Her heart, no longer *Red* enough.

The attic was filled with paper monuments,
including their canceled checks we could finally shred.
I kept some of those memories.

Mom and Dad died not in *Black*.
Mom and Dad died in the *Black*.
Mortgages, two, paid in full.
Money in the bank for grown kids.
Thankful there was no *Red* at the end,
except for Mom's *Bright Red* dress,   funeral roses,
           and some of her BIC pens.

Dad's Fourth Quarter Pass

Sitting near his wise wingback chair,
at home with Dad, football, and male codes.
Football Sunday in our family living room.
"What does a quarterback really do?"
"Patsy, just watch. Stop asking so many questions."
Dad expected me to learn mostly by watching.

Sometimes chairs are at bedsides.
Livid just looking at wall clocks.
Mocking me. Mocking us.
Forcing me to teleport one more time to a Browns game.
A win or lose Cleveland thing.

My latest reverie about winning playoff tickets just for Dad and me
halted momentarily while nice nurses take turns
coming in and out of our cuckoo clock.
The doctor, skilled locksmith repairing in other rooms.
Finally arrives with *Hope,* nothing more.
Hospitals filled with only *Hope* make anyone ready for more morphine.

Hope sat in the room with us all day.
Then Dad's faltering breath kept telling her to go away.
Hope could not take away the gray air.
Hope could not take away his renal failure.
Hope could not stop Dad's prostate cancer from metastasizing.
Hope could not take away Dad, lying there still and silent
like he was already pronounced dead.
No longer able to even whisper my name.
Hope could not keep me from falling asleep
right before Dad died.
Yes, I cried, unable to say *Goodbye*
while he was at least somewhat alive.

Doctors say concerned fathers often slip away.
I imagine Dad sat in his chair one last time while his slow
breaths lulled me. Lullabied me to sleep right before.
Not surprised Dad needed to be Dad that afternoon.
Filling me with team spirit.
Enough to become our family's new quarterback.

Apartment Living

Unusual loves sitting next to the usual. Never let someone into your life, even with a front entrance key. In apartment buildings, impossible.

I.

The words rattled in his throat
at least twice that night.
"Where's your bitch-ass mother?"

His voice almost in my living room,
sitting on the couch with me.
Where was this husband, father,
brother, temporary live-in lover,
a *Baby Daddy* delivering
his impromptu podcast on blast?

From his balcony?
Lying in wait outside?
For the mother he wanted to choke?
What did she do to make him
breathe fire like that?
Why always blame the woman?

II.

Indistinguishables. Mumblings.
Many who were half asleep
awakened now.
By ticking clocks of their own?
Another reason to move out?
Thoughts ready to go back to sleep.
Got to go to work early!
SHUT THE FXXX UP!!!!!

III.

Our building's parking lot
usually quiet. Except the day

police cars careened through,
blockading the usual.
Caught the *perp*. Quick work.
A car thief? A drug dealer?
A bail jumper?
No one ever said.
Saw them handcuff him.
Regrouped. Sped.
Parked our cars in solitude again.

IV.

Apartment living!
Elevator One not working again!
New tenants gifted everyone roaches.
Clear your kitchen cabinets.
Exterminators coming Tuesday.

Custodial staff worker fixed my toilet.
Young. Black Suicide. Used his own shotgun.
Bragged about his little son
just the other day!

V.

A dead body in one of the stairwells once.
No one ever said why. Just another lie?

A match thrown down the trash compactor.
Another angry tenant easing pain?
Not a completely tall tale.

Evacuated by a piercing
sound that could have waked
that dead woman in the stairwell.

We stood away from the building
in various degrees of discomfort,
forced to wear slippers and robes
we usually keep to ourselves.

Saw strangers who must be neighbors.
Finally speaking out of necessity
or sheer boredom.

VI.

He was no longer there.
A tenant who barricaded himself
in the gun shop down the street.

Confused gunfire took him down.
Made local news.
A Vietnam Vet.
Management said he was one of us.
Not "Homeless."
"Harmless."

His blank eyes scared more than one of us.
He sat in our lobby for hours.
No one was supposed to sit there.
Sympathy broke the rules for him.
His elderly mother grieved alone.

One LAST DROP of BLOOD

In a very clean bathroom stall.
In solemn silence before sitting down.
Inside my community church.
It happened.
Felt God was laughing.
Not loud enough for derision.
Prayerfully making sure.
Quickly pulling down pants.
Introspecting my panties.
Looking for stains.
Something we women
learn how to do very fast.
Forced in solitary confinement.
Forced to always remember
to carry pads and Motrin
before those times
fill me with regret.
Recalling days of absence
doubled over in my bed.
Since age 11.

 CHOOSING NOT TO TRY ANYMORE   to   HAVE CHILDREN.
Flash forward again, that very fickle trickle is   FINAL.   FEELS FATAL.

No more familiar clumps or clots.
A spurt of blood I must notice.
Streaming down my right leg.
Streams no more.

THAT   ONE   LAST   DROP
    WAVED   A   FIRM GOODBYE.

Catching my fleeting fire
with the softest tissue.

               WOMB   ALREADY   FELT   USELESS.

No homilies could
stop Stigmata on wrists, hands, or feet.
A dull pain in my stomach.

       Another FLASH of DEATH.   A Very Painful   SIGNAL.
           M-E-N-O-P-A-U-S-E!   An   E N DING.
                 BUT NOT MY OWN.   That day,

       I DIED AGAIN   to   LIVE AGAIN.

BARE FEET

"Earth's crammed with heaven,
And every common bush afire with God,
But only he who sees, takes off his shoes;
The rest sit round and pluck blackberries."

—Elizabeth Barrett Browning, *Aurora Leigh*

Tower City Kiss
for EY

He lived at the top.
Building One, ninth floor.
Top of the city,
he kissed me!

One. More to remember.
His lips. Playful.
Yet tender.
Knew I was a widow.

Not my husband.
A longtime friend.
His kiss. More to remember
against the wall.
Lingering close to his door.

Cleave Land. The Land.
Still my Believeland.
City of Light!
This kind man finally kissing me
against this backdrop.
Spectacular movie skyline.
Terminal Tower.
Tower City illumination.
Wanting his landmark kisses that night.
Not his landmark achievements.

Night touching our desires through
the balcony window.
Stars a million lightning bugs
willfully captured. Glowing.
Glowing in waiting jars just for us
at night. That night.

No turning off bright lights.
No penthouse seduction.
No removals of clothing.
No clumsy departures.
Kissing was right/tight that night.

Shush!
Response Poem to "Hero" by Jericho Brown

I always had something to say even when Momma shushed me.
She taught me to put my thoughts and feelings into conch shells.
They looked beautiful. Bright, unbroken on the outside.
She did it for me, herself
and Daddy, tired all the time.
Factory workers appreciate silence.
Slept during the day.
Ate dinner past 9 PM with us in the breakfast nook.
We felt his presence, but he did not talk much then.

Shush in every cell of my home
felt like
solitary confinement.
No light for at least a day.
Not even a shaft of it coming from cracks in the ceiling.
Especially when I said something my parents
forbade me to say.

No need for swear jars.
Every morning brushing teeth
with special toothpaste called "Young Ladies Don't Complain."
Never forgetting to gargle with Listerine
rinsing out the unspoken.

Never meaning no disrespect.
No sassing my elders or teachers.
Just trying to think for myself
beyond amens, psalms,
textbooks, and televisions.

Got whipped one day with a twig fetched from the Maple tree.
Those twigs really hurt!
Got welts.
We called them, "Whep marks."
Ended up with sparse red bumps that
stood tall amid the faint lines on both my forearms.
The following day, we concealed my mutiny.

Wore long sleeves to school.
No one knew as we read *Dick and Jane* in our groups.
      Mom said, "You moved around like grease in one of my skillets.
           Put your arms in the way too much!"

I should have just stood there with my skinny self.
Steady and obedient, ready to walk single file to another school assembly.
None of us got beat like Kunta Kente brought back after running away.
Never wanted whippings, even slight ones again
for my runaway thoughts about equality and other stuff.

Learned to keep them inside those shells
at least for a while.
Save them in poems and journals.
Momma taught me about writing. Wrote herself.
I kept her creations after she died.
Hope one day to publish them,
also more of mine.

                Shush!
       For now.   Not forever.
      Work 9 to 5 like our Daddies, we must!
                Shush!
    Put thoughts and feelings into more crevices
      giving *THEM* right or wrong power over us
              Just shush!
    Screaming inside mouths duct-taped shut.
              Just Shush!

Different Drums, Different Songs

Migraines hide in orchestra pits.
Dodging suns and shadows.
Sneak. Play all the instruments.
Hear the drums in our heads.
Misdiagnosed just like White Women.
Ignored by *Maestros*.
Black Migraines rarely play in first or
second chairs.

Believe my snare drum started in our car.
Loved riding with parents, three siblings.
Me, hating the motion.
Felt like the *rat tat tatting* might make me throw up.
My other travel companions
sometimes helped.
A brown paper bag.
Peppermints in Mom's purse.

Mind triggers enumerating as I grew.
The orchestra jubilantly playing
the familiar refrains.
Hair spray on my wet hair refusing to dry.
Inescapable dust everywhere.
On furniture. Tables. Ceilings.
Storage rooms anxious to leave
unwanted presents in my nostrils.
No windows to open at work.
No fresh air anywhere.

Ever-increasing dissonant sounds
intensified by menacing sunlight
blazing into my synapses.
Heard bongos. Congas.
Then bass drums accompanied
by intermittent cymbals and tambourines.
Ever-present needling cello strings
sustaining my stressed-out pain!
Accumulating Bad Brain Days.
Using up well-earned sick leave.

The beginning? The ending?
Hoped. Never expected.
Too-familiar throbbing
headache melody circling all around me.
Then temporary, frightening
Blindness in one eye or both?
Hoping for just blurriness.
Enough to see at least the accompanist.

Imagine growing up like that?
Imagine trying to learn like that?
Imagine teaching like that?
Imagine walking like that?
Imagine driving like that?
Imagine living another day like that?
Necessary unsafe measures.

Diagnosed: Allergic to *Dust. Mold.
Cigarette Smoke*. Anticipating
another dark bedroom day,
Hope came like magic
in a hypodermic needle
filled with *I am desperate*,
won't ask what.
Was he just an ENT
or self-proclaimed herbalist savior?
Injected me separate times.
Once. Twice. Possibly thrice.
No more.
Those *Drums!*
That debilitating orchestra, gone!

Finally! Welcome!
My Orchestra!
My Drums!
My Songs!

Grendels, My Modern Epic Poem

Prologue

Please do not gobble me!
Stop acting like Grendel pursuing Beowulf.
Stop stalking me like the Giant after Jack!
Or the Cyclops who tried to defeat Odysseus.
Some tales can become Grimm very fast!
Let's first talk about me, me, me, and me.
Then end with cleanliness.

Once upon a time, there was a kid.
Correction: a curious kid.
Correction: a curious Black kid
trying to live her simple American life.
Correction: simple Black American life.
But nothing about life or being me is ever simple!
Especially when you are Black!
Trying to be, just be little me.
Not belittled me.

Part 1: Crayons

A Black kid who loved to draw
life with all her crayons
but once gave most away
to her classmates when they asked.
By the end of the school year,
she was left with only two significant colors.
Black and Yellow.
Forced to color life with just two colors.
Never enough!
Glad she still had her Black crayon!

Even the kids who borrowed
never let her borrow back
what clearly belonged to her!
I guess kids learn quickly
how to keep things
only for themselves.

Was she tired of asking
or too shy to keep asking?
Too late, the teacher invoked another rule.
"Do not loan your supplies to anyone!"
The desks had lids that did not lock!
Deemed teacher's new rule pointless.

Part 2: Miss Tyranny

The beginning of any child's night terrors!
Being laughed at in class.
Wrote my first original poem at age nine.
Miss Armstrong, mean old-maid White tyrant.
Cruelty with stick legs.
Made all of us stand in front,
one at a time sometimes,
to read aloud.
That day, I dug my grave's hole deep.
I was proud to read my poem aloud.
Then she started the laugh track.
Said something like,
"You call that a poem?
Go sit down!"
Prolonging my agony
whenever she could.

I was the best student
she probably ever had!
Everyone knew.
Despite her looks. Her words.
Her racist shovel she used quite often.
Especially for me!
My confidence, overconfidence
had remained high. Until that day.

This callous teacher encouraged
everyone to embarrass me.
Discourage me from writing my own story.
Made me play *Imposter Syndrome* top-ten
records, even into my twenties.
I kept writing anyway.

Part 3: Mr. Tyranny

In middle school
(we called it "junior high"),
Mr. T, my White Social Studies teacher,
a thoughtless green man announced
my IQ during class.
Said I was an overachiever.
Asked a Black male student
who was smarter than the average Bear,
"Why aren't you getting *As* like Marlana?"

Was Mr. T simply calling me a stupid Black person?
A stupid Black? Or just a stupid female,
never supposed to outshine a Black male? Any male?
Far exceeding his expectations?
Was he telling me to be Dumbo
for the rest of my existence?
Singled out again.
In the highest school section.
The highest track. I did not clapback.

Whatever his purpose,
my young heart knew.
My private stuff should not be posted
on a bulletin board or passed out
like a test paper in class.
I was just a preteen. A kid
wishing to go hide in a bathroom stall.
No lawsuit followed that day.
My pen to paper did.

Part 4: Grendels Wearing Sheep's Clothing

In Catholic high school, my Grendels
pretended they liked my kind.
Allowed me to be smarter than most,
mainly because I was a *Sleeper*.
The White nuns didn't see my sleeping car coming.
Once they did, all sorts of yellow tape
blocked my path.

They let me be a sophomore writer.
Until they had to make the school newspaper   disappear.
I was heir apparent. Next editor-in-chief.
But everyone before me was White.
Headline never printed:
**"We Will Never Have
a Black Editor-in-Chief Named Marlana."**
No more high school newspaper called
The Spectrum. They refused to honor its name.
I kept on writing anyway.

Part 5: Stained-Glass Sinners

My high school transcript is still screaming, "Injustice!" Still wishing she could take the stand to testify on my behalf. Talk about despicable White-collar crimes. What about those committed while wearing habits and collars? Sitting near stained-glass windows?

"Salutatorian? Marlana was really Number One in her class!"
Once my former classmates read this, there will be grimaces and gasps.

I was Smart,   but Black and Non-Catholic.   Some still say I am.
      Who were my Grendels then?   Repeat Offenders.
Even the graduation program
yelled out in protest.
No truth serums during the ceremony.
No valid Lie Detector tests.
No Prayer Circles surrounding me.

No confessionals made nuns confess
why they made those drastic alterations.
Why they cut my fabric so easily.
Divine Mercy made sure one of my
challenged grades' stitching was corrected.
Underneath, a threadbare, concealed scandal.
Indisputable proof went undetected until too late.
Not even before Mass and graduation.

      White Matriarchy. White Patriarchy. White Privilege.
      All worked hand-in-hand to hand me
      second-best, second-class citizen, Silver.
      Not my well-deserved, earned
      Gold.

I stood there on the stage in my White, head to toe.
Clarity by my side. Realized it was there later.
I was no longer wearing the robe I had worn before.
I never blamed all the nuns. I never blamed all the priests.
Never blamed Mother Mary. NEVER blamed God!
I blame *Boulders. Monoliths. Cauldrons. Cancers.*
          Catholic Guilt. All those closed the school one year later.

Before and after that, double shifts prayed
my family would
NEVER hire a lawyer. We never did.
My parents wore Timex. Not Rolex.
Besides, statutes of limitations
fly out of windows early.

Silver linings are still inside my altered clothing.
My intelligence. My excellence. My confidence.
My honors. My grants. My scholarships.
My friends. My family. My faith. My GOLD.

The Almighty is always there with mending threads.   Alleluia!   Amen.

Part 6: The Moral

All those Grendel armies
kept coming after me.
My whole family:
My mother.
My father.
My two sisters.
My little brother!
Coming after us because
we were the wrong bothersome color
in their Crayola boxes.

All of our Black lives!
Telling us to only think what *They* Think.
Telling us to only do what *They* Do.
Telling us when to speak. When not to speak.
Telling us to eat. When not to eat.
Telling us to sleep. When not to sleep.
Telling us not to vote.

Telling us not to write.
Telling us to never believe.
Not in our miracles or magic.
Somehow, we still do.

Not hating our Grendels.
More what they represent.
If we refused to comply,
ever refused to pretend to be Grendels ourselves,
they abruptly came at us with their claws.
Chased all of us into the woods.
Tried to make us their dinner.
Always attempting to eat each of us whole.

But Grendels never liked how we tasted.
Spewed us out pretty much intact.
We hated the slime and stench left on our bodies.
Not easy to scrub off all at once.
Not easy to forget.
We learned a lot about how to clean
ourselves thoroughly, limb by limb, regularly.
Doing it better every time.
I always use my favorite cleanser — Words.

Watermelon
for my sister, Jameela

Sister,
soul throwing ideas, words, other entities
around before Naomi Campbell could box.
Before cannons underestimated quick, quiet power.
Doing more than wearing an Afro in the 60s,
Jameela made us new food.
Lentil soup and other exotic dishes only
little sister fully enjoyed. Wanted recipes,
not her exteriors or religious choices.
Both believing and praying,
never openly proselytizing one another,
Jameela's Methodist became Sunni.

Sole sibling,
soul grasping change by his lapels,
Jameela bakes bread now in a spacious kitchen.
She loves kneading acres of soil, more than I do.
Even pulling weeds midday in classrooms
risking to breed respect, growth, sometimes (by accident) admiration.
in hearts and minds, always mine.
Scattering acceptance amid dissension.
Calm in spite of rejection's vexing
laughter, walking away,
labeling our crazy ways.
The Perfect English
even interests in Smothers Brothers, Beatles, Blues, and Opera
or my college love of WMMS. Cat Stevens. Joe Cocker.
In post-racial America, what exactly is a White-Black sister or brother anyway?

And are we finally proud of America today?

Years ago,
in Sacramento,
visiting Jameela and her brood.
Coming back through some hilly meandering
When flat tires interrupt buoyant moods.
I even have a photo of Dad bending down to fix things again.

Pictures of family
harvesting together in
Jameela's community garden.

But that's not the part remembered most.
Jameela has no recall.
It's when some of *Them*,
not *Us*, came driving by,
glaring, especially at Jameela's hijab.
Scarf that makes her sweat, look like a nun.
A lady once asked if she was one.
I was there.
Shocked?
Jameela is used to people staring.
Saying things
about terrorism and threats. Bombs.
Or always being plucked for random searches at airports.
This was before that though.
They cruised, pausing near us,
sun as hot as high noon.
Almost on cue,
Jameela reached into our rental.
Then held one of the watermelons plucked from harvest.
Held it high as Excalibur,
then brandished it.
A watermelon of all things,
brandished as a fist though,
not a sword or a gun.
The disarmed simply had to whir away.

Not always.

Sullivan's Island: July 2003

Where are our ancestors?
In tide or sky?
In seashells that crack to touch?
Red, blue kites carefree at midday.
Beach towels warming mindlessness.
Walkways toasting forgetfulness.
In laughter of oblivious children
hiding their bodies in sand.

Remembrances are pest control engulfing sailboats and shores.
Bouncing off the safety of gentrified mansions
and restaurants named after Poe.
We looked for our legacies,
signs amid the unexpected:
Keep Out. Private Property. Do Not Litter. Clean Up after Your Dog.

Spent two days searching for our ancestors' **WELCOME** signs
only to find
two brothas riding rims of a garbage truck,
part of the few of us with the realtors' permission,
and the lonely marker near Fort Moultrie.
A Black park ranger (who used to live on Sullivan's Island)
showed us what's hiding from everyone's sight.

Sad, cheated,
strangely renewed, I took photographs.
Words and photograph remembrances.
On the beach,
wrote prayers in the sand to cast away
imposing structures and bodies.
We entered spirits.
Clasped brothas and sistas long gone,
the true, eternal owners of this *Property*.

After I made monuments in mind and sand,
I was propelled. Spirits told me to walk,
anoint my bare feet
in the Atlantic Ocean.

The water crystallized, called me
to embrace the past with my whole soul.
Truly face it.
Sullivan's Island,
still a hallowed place.
Will never be erased
by shallow people and shallow spaces.

We All Need to Wade in that Water!

This Is a Man's World

"This is a man's world, this is a man's world
But it wouldn't be nothing, nothing without a woman or a girl"

— **James Brown & Betty Jean Newsome,**
"It's a Man's, Man's, Man's World"

Part 1

In long-distance relationships,
every phone conversation is an imprint upon spirits.
Forgetting to call me is worth a police interrogation
or at least a press conference.
Yes, you forewarned me about your disappearing acts.
How I might be inclined to ask, "Where did he go?"

Even after all our marathon phone conversations
talking about unpredictable Cleveland weather and agreeable Los Angeles.
God, astrology, Obama, snow, earthquakes,
you interject how you like full lips, apple bottoms, and PDAs.
Your favorite color is *Yellow*.
You like brie cheese, Cabernet Sauvignon, and Indonesian cigarettes.
But would give up the latter for me.
You listen and record me, too.
We laugh.
Share secrets.
Talk about kissing for the first time. Being together.

Sometimes sweaty talk comes in torrents.
Now this drought of words.
Waiting to embrace your sigh again.
I try to play my part,
yet tears encourage me
to call you to "Bless you out!"
Voicemail announces your name.
Sounds like a *Blade Runner* replicant,
not my sweetie.
Hanging up.
Frustration assailed by *Courage*.
Courage that pushes my lips on the second attempt.

Uttering words of conciliation, not *Anger*.
An hour. A day. Possibly a week before your sigh comes back
with the apologies and detailed explanations
I choose to accept.

Part 2

My parents were married for almost 60 years.
Both died in 2005.
Mom in February. Dad in July.
My father NEVER LET
my mother drive while he was in the car.
She was an excellent driver, excellent mother, too.
I always knew why Mom
never complained about being deprived —
because she chose for her small children sitting in the back:
three females and one male.
Even odds were never even.
Not for families like mine.
So even when Dad got us lost temporarily,
he stayed at the wheel.
No one ever complained.

My Concrete Heart

My heart can no longer live in concrete.
Places where I cannot cry out loud,
not even through the cracks.
Places where my clothes no longer fit into my drawers.
That small bathroom my late husband used one last time.
Shower faucet still dripped long after he died.
Over 17 years! Longer than we were married!

My two-bedroom rental, where walls kept whispering
about dreams I tried not to remember.
Places where my hands never felt warm
forced me to stay home another day from a job and friends.
Should have canceled those subscriptions long ago.

                                                          My lease finally up.
                                         In a cheap motel for close to a week.
                                  Did not see any roaches waiting with me.
                       Only me waiting for a plane to my new Arizona home.
                                            No more economy seats.
                                    Flew first class. First time. Deserved it.
                    Toasty white towels for my grateful face and hands.
                                       The tight restroom, a palace.

                                   Marked in my mind. My parents' graves.
                                       Marvin's, too. The miscarriage.
                                Finally moving from the only places,
                                     the mazes that had kept me
                                             standing petrified.
                                             Yet I already knew.

Looking from
my window seat,
my breath different
above the concrete.

The clouds still clouds.
I'm alone, but never alone.
I already see verdant terrain below me
where the heartbeats that will sustain me wait.

Tasting Rainbows
for Black Families

Skittles are Trayvon Martins.
A bright array of colors asking
us to let them enjoy their innocence.
Their crunchy sweetness.
Asking us to allow them to be
in any neighborhood they
choose to be.
Late at night with their bags
and flashlights.
Ready to rob residents only
of their candy happiness.

Teachers like me know Trayvons.
Love seeing them in our schools.
Tell them not to wear hoodies up
in our classrooms. Must follow our rules.
Treat them on good days. Holidays.
Halloweens. Reese's cups.
Big kids love being Skittles BEST.
We should be happy they still do.
They would be Skittles forever
if America would let them.

So, why scatter our Skittles
all over our pavements?
With no chance to taste the rainbows.
    All the greens,

        yellows,

           oranges,

            purples,

              REDS!

              Brilliance gone in one massive gulp.

Nina Simone, High Priestess of Our Souls

Goddess of Liberty
and Love,
you put gold chains
on our hearts.
Around our necks.
Around our souls.
Not just for raiment.
Mainly to save us.
Goddess of generous lips,
dark skin, bright turbans,
and brave Afro picks,
keep sprinkling sage into our lives.

You are a New Cassandra.
People believe when you sing
in our homes. On podcasts.
On soundtracks. On televisions.
Still keepin' it real. On IG reels.
Still testifying posthumously
about bad romances. Lies. Betrayals.
Our Sister Sadie silences. Our white noise.
Our civil rights in spite of incivilities.
Our stagnating rivers of inequality.

Nina, you are silk and stone.
Beauty and backbone.
Ballads and anthems.
A Sojourner, deftly
passing down tablets
filled with truth. With wisdom.
Never to be ignored.
Transmitted to us
through your body of songs.
Both your voice and fingers
still electrify Steinways.
You are still a powerful nation
helping build other nations.

Nina. Yes, you saw reasons
Americans should leave
to be revered overseas.
Helped sisters and brothers,
escape words like, "Ugly."
Nina, you knew all about derision.
White folks with their false diagrams.
Underrating all our talents.
Even our inventions.

Nina, invented a new world order
never afraid to dress to be heard.
Clothing speaking aloud. Got louder.
Got prouder of our ancestors.
Started wearing our Afros
with more splendor.
Never surrender.
Keep singing freedom songs
with Nina leading.
Singing about Our Holocausts.
Those Bitten,   Battered,   BOMBED,   **MURDERED**.

    Never forget **Our Lists   Injustice** writes for us.
   We have folks living in Mississippi!   Who still can't even vote!
          DAMN!

Nobody but Nina had visions to see and be heard.
Her keys and contralto committed,
still awakened like Dizzy's trumpet.
Resounding from North to South.   South to North.
The Carolinas.   The Carolinas to the Mississippis.
      Battlefields still,   near and far.

    Violence still slaying non-violence.
       DAMN!!!
Memphis,   **Birmingham,**   **Montgomery,**   **Selma!**
     Nina always sang.

Wish I could finally shout about new days like Nina.   Sing "Feeling Good."
  No Codas yet.   **MISSISSIPPI GODDAM!!!**

   Our High Priestess must keep singing.
   Nina Simone, High Priestess of Our Souls.

Dear Thomas Jefferson

We're taking the knee, Thomas Jefferson.
Chief architect of that D-O-C.
1776 genius heralded in show tunes.
Long been time to put away our
pickaninny baskets filled with hot dogs,
hamburgers, barbecue delicacies,
lemonade, and textbook sides.
Never healthy. That annual diet of grilled lies.

Hard to still wave flags, pledge allegiances,
march in unison.
Play fife and drum songs of John Philip Sousa.
Or love fireworks on Independence Day.
Or hear y'all's forefathers speaking on our money,
daily reminders of how much we owe you.
Forgetting how much y'all still owe us!

You and your homies still peering
down on us regular folk.
All the way from Mount Rushmore.
All high like gods on Olympus.
Fathering us for centuries upon centuries in
ways that curl anyone's hair into ponytails
or turn it white overnight!
Some still sing praises about the other two.
Not slaveholders like your Patriot George and you!

We must take the knee for Sally.
All Sallys. Several knees.
Pretenses are petticoats. Parasols long out of style.
Servant, not your wife, on an extended Paris honeymoon
still slaving in your Monticello bedrooms.
Sarah "Sally" Hemings, mother of the secret six,
deliberately not counted in your egg carton.
Your champions still bludgeoning CRT.
The 1619 Project.
DNA tired of perpetrating
lies still lying in y'all's forefathers' beds.

We must take several knees, Thomas and Company.
Reclaim our legacies.
Find our stories' privileged pens, like yours.

> *Still Tar. Feather. Brand. Chain. Mutilate. Pillory. Rape.*
> *Still hide White flesh on Black family trees.*
> *Trees y'all, so many, tried to cut down.*
> *Burned like Salem witches in our forests.*
> *Buried deep, deep, deep in the ground.*
>
> *OUR BRAVE PENS ALWAYS DIG DEEPER!*

My Babies

Everything swells when a
woman is pregnant.
Mini Michelin ankles.
Buxom breasts.
Waistlines so big and bodacious.
Such beauty, bumping into someone
without really bumping, or
feeling the bump of your first child.
Feet anxious to touch your skin against theirs.

I never got those sensations,
because fate gave me a misfiring cannon.
Better known as a miscarriage.
I read somewhere that the hospital
might still be able to tell a would-be mother
if it would have been a boy or a girl.

                    What good would knowing do?
                    What good would knowing do?

Dreaming about your child
that never was or will be is like pounding
your heart and soul with a meat cleaver.

Moot point. The doctors said it was
too early to tell.
High-risk me failed at the truest test
of my womanhood. Or did I?
Looking at my lemonade,
my breasts are still bigger.
The lemons?
My waist will always bulge.
Ask my belts for air.
Cankles? I guess I always had those.

I make the most delicious lemonade babies.
Immaculately conceived.
No sperm clinics needed.
I keep my babies in my special NICUs.

My spiral binders and manila folders.
My legal pads. My phone notes.
My laptop savior who saved me and my words.
My babies call to me in the morning and at night.
I nourish and revise them once
I swaddle them in my arms.
Give them lots of water and sunlight,
so Jimmy, Joanie, and their siblings
will grow strong limbs.
Tell them they are smarter than smartphones every day.
Play Duke Ellington's "Take the A Train" on blast
for them and for me.

Much older now,
overjoyed about still giving birth.
Actually, more and more and more.
No surrogates needed.
Not ever. Just me.
God's plan, awake in wee hours.
Losing sleep I can never regain.
My arms are not angry.
They are happy
and full of Hallelujah Praise Dances
awaiting more deliveries.

Remembering Cleveland Snow

"Take me back to subtle snowfall on busy streets
where I would experience snowflakes greeting me, kissing me
softly for the first time."

—Kimiko White, "Hoboken, New Jersey"

2014, my baby brother Wiley died.   A heart attack.   A massive loss.
A vivid reminder   of the last time   I saw Cleveland snow.
Well below zero snow.
Not the soft kind.
Flakes falling,   slipping through my knit gloves   and
frozen fingertips.
Leaving a moist film on my lips.   Almost feels like a comforting kiss.
Almost feels like feathers or silk   gently touching me. Fooling me
into spring.
That light snow, never firm enough
for me to revisit childhood
to make a smiling snowman,
not even a playful snowball. Or full angel wings.

Bitter Cleveland snow in January can blind us.
Bury us.   Bury anything.   Timberland boots.   Stalled cars.

Even feelings.

Used to make me stay home for days.
Cozying up to a recalcitrant space heater
when the apartment building's furnace failed.
My pilled white blanket reminding me
what still waits ready to diverge our paths through parking lots.
I curl, fall asleep on that solemn sofa.
Only leaving home for groceries.
Hoping they will last   and last   and last.
Last long enough to forget.

Coax thick icicles down with a broom.
Wait until heaving, heavy white snow
on the rooftop crashes over back gutters.
Bends and unhinges things.

Then, the ghosts will slowly, silently melt away.
Seems like they do.
Remember, in blustery Cleveland winters,

Lake Erie needs time to put lots of icing on remaining birthday cakes.
Shifting into stranger and stranger shapes.

Ice will take its time thawing.
Will take its time thawing.
Will take its time thawing.

1992, my husband died in January.   Diabetes.
In Cleveland.
Never let our grief become glaciers.

Talford Family Home Epitaph

Why didn't anyone call the police? Or call me?

They stole from my Talford Family home. Shamelessly. Took what many thieves crave, like diamonds, our copper wire. Poked holes in innocent walls. Spread ugliness over happy childhoods and adult spaces. Rummaged it to pieces. Felt like they left spittle and feces on our memories.

Who do we blame when desperate people
ransack, clamoring for their lottery ticket or crack money
at our address?

Violate homes. Violate homeowners when they're not even home. They took the refrigerator! We know someone saw them. One of the streetlights announced them because it shines right onto our driveway.

But I guess that old "snitches get stitches" mantra
had become everyone's in my old, less friendly neighborhood.

So I flew back home as fast as I could. The security door was broken. Side door unhinged by the missing refrigerator.

Survivor's guilt.

Should have reinstalled the ADT system after our dear brother, last to reside there, died. Guess my grief was the real thief.

Or did they steal that, too?

Our house was ruined! A frame of what it used to be. Someone left unsightly graffiti. It took me four more years to clean it out. Even with help. The local Salvation Army was happy to see me. I drove up several times in my rented Chevy. That was 2018. The year our Talford Family home finally sold to the highest bidder. A price far less than its worth. But sometimes, the memories remind us that money is just money. I stood next to our stalwart maple tree in the backyard, so big it seemed to be talking to the clouds, God, and me. Leaned against it and sighed.

Prayed. Then finally said, "Goodbye."

Flight Lessons

> "Hold fast to dreams
> For if dreams die
> Life is a broken-winged bird
> That cannot fly."
>
> **—Langston Hughes, "Dreams"**

Langston Hughes still perches on Harlem stoops.
Once a Cleveland fledgling at Central High.
Now our play daddy or gentle uncle
sheltering us with his glorious word wings.
Traveling. Traveling with flocks sometimes.
Carrying our bigger than big bounteous nest dreams,
giving us large wingspans to soar
higher than wandering albatrosses.
Giving us courage to safely fly
across seas, oceans, continents, like him.
Like our ancestors.

Langston Hughes still gives flight lessons
to many kids who grew up like me.
Cleveland sparrows, robins, cardinals.
My fast friends.
Watching. Reading.
Curiosity traveling.
Befriending more feathered sisters,
brothers. Learning how to fly
without leaving neighborhoods.
Not even the maple trees.

Langston Hughes still gives us new friends.
Arizona cardinals. Quails. Woodpeckers.
Roadrunners, no longer mere cartoons.
New wished-for best bird friends.
Grocery shopping for poems in my new backyard.
Specially hummingbirds. Colored beauties
gathering morning nectar
from gregarious, voluminous aloe veras.

Langston Hughes, still the ultimate hummingbird.
Resplendent, respected.
Moving meticulously very fast!
Defying motion.
Forward, backward,
upside-down fabulous verses.
Unfettered flight frenzies.
Fearlessly giving effortless manna.
Morning mantras for freedom everywhere.

Langston Hughes, also our ragtag pigeon poet.
With never-forget-our-gray bird stanzas.
Grayness still lives in Harlem,
Cleveland, Phoenix, LA
Everywhere!

Pigeons overhead now. Flying high
with other bird friends
across seas, oceans, continents.
Spikes on eaves shoo nuisances.
Won't stop funky vanilla milkshake messes.
Uncleanliness we keep trying to forget.
Still flying high.
Everywhere!

Remember. Always remember —
All birds
wanted/unwanted must be!
Let them flutter on our pages.
Everywhere!

Erasure Poem: The Black National Anthem

▇▇▇▇▇▇▇▇▇▇▇

Till earth and heaven ring.
▇▇▇▇▇▇▇▇▇▇▇▇▇▇▇ Liberty;
▇▇▇▇ rejoicing rise,
High as ▇▇▇▇▇▇ skies,
▇▇▇▇▇▇▇▇▇▇▇▇▇▇ rolling sea.
▇▇▇▇▇▇▇▇▇▇▇▇▇▇▇▇▇ the dark past ▇▇ taught us,
▇▇▇▇▇▇▇▇▇▇▇▇▇▇▇▇▇▇▇ the present ▇▇ brought us;
Facing the rising sun ▇▇▇▇▇▇▇▇▇▇▇▇▇
Let us march on ▇▇▇▇▇▇▇▇▇▇

Stony ▇▇▇▇▇▇▇▇▇
Bitter ▇▇▇▇▇▇▇▇▇▇▇
▇▇▇▇▇▇ days ▇▇▇▇ hope ▇▇▇ ▇▇▇
▇▇ with a steady beat,

▇▇▇▇▇▇▇ our weary feet,
Come ▇▇▇▇ place for ▇▇▇▇ our fathers ▇▇▇▇▇

Lyrics from elyrics.net.

Why Do We Still Sing Those Songs?

Slave songs remind us — Bind us.
Four little girls sitting in church pews. Was it Sunday School?
Probably reading their Bibles
reciting prayers parents taught them
before that hate bomb detonated **MORE HATE!**

Four innocent little Birmingham girls:
Addie Mae, Cynthia, Carol, and Carole once sang
those songs filled with words that had little meaning to them as kids.
They died before they ever   learned the painful connotations
and the misery still lying on Egypt's soil.   In Jerusalem.   In America.
Right next door.
Dark skins eviscerated by unforgiving cancers
with common *KKK* names like Bob.

More innocent little Southern girls like Ruby Bridges   Northern girls.
Western. Eastern.
All Black kids still singing those songs in schools
with closed windows and shutters. Same old segregated melodies.
   After busing, we are grown. Still Singing.

Of rivers to cross in our divided communities.
Of hills to overcome needing more than meager trekking poles.
Of places we should never speak about or go to alone at night.
Of forgiving trespasses and trespassers in our daily prayers.
Those who brought our ancestors here damaged.
Whose descendants are still not handled with care.
Yet we still say, The Lord's Prayer. Still say, "Forgive our trespassers."
   Should we ever forgive?

Our bondage is bondage with far too many tomes. Pages upon pages filled with too much extrapolated data and too many definitions for our diseases, deaths, murders, and suicide ideations served up with lower-cased excuses instead of the **Bold-faced facts**. Finally acknowledge the perpetrators and the victims of these crimes. Give us all the multiple meanings in the next Merriam-Webster. Finally post it everywhere! Then finally, give us **OUR BOLD-FACED FREEDOMS!**

Brothers and Sisters, still writing poems? Then another. Then another. Then Another????   Keep writing.   Still not enough.

Our best poems? STILL OUR SLAVE SONGS!
Singing those songs, all day and night, throughout the years
has taught us how to live and die here.
Lie in our caskets with courage and pride.
Still facing *the rising sun of a new day begun*. Hoping for a very long time.
Still hoping for more days than Inhumanity has stolen from us.

So, we sing another sacred slave song. Please teach our children how to sing.
Daily Reminding us—Binding our past with our present, and our futures.
KEEP SINGING.   *We Shall Overcome*.
 KEEP SINGING.   *Go Down Moses*.
  KEEP SINGING.   *His Eye is on the Sparrow*.
   KEEP SINGING.   *Wade in the Water*.
    KEEP SINGING.   *The Black National Anthem*.
**KEEP SINGING.   KEEP SINGING.   KEEP SINGING.
TILL VICTORY IS WON!**

My Superbad Head of Hair

My hair has been dyed, fried, petrified.
Yet never pulled until last week.
Like the space was too
small. So some degree
of yanking was necessary.
Fondling it for a minute
not satisfying enough for you?

No hair follicles yelled out in agony.
They stayed in my scalp heaven.
Enjoying the oils in a Roman bath.
No, not a flirtation, not coitus. Not an orgy.
Why do people having sex
think pulling hair is *Sexy?*
The pleasure and pain *Narrative.*
Would I ever participate in that?

Pull my hair in public.
Wonder how *Spooks* feel?
Standing. Not sitting by the door.
Violation. Humiliation. The first. The last
words I am spelling.
In my **Biggest, Baddest PAM GRIER VOICE!**
Ready to shoot a hole in a wall.
Trying to avoid criminal acts,
I karate chop bar stools.
Anything inanimate that hurts.

I am a BLACK WOMAN —
A BIG BADASSSSSS Action Shero with a tight Fro.
I run this joint PURRFECTLY.

My Rules should **NEVER** be broken.

Please Don't Call Me "Marla"

I am not that throwaway ex-wife
of that ex-President
many women like me would love
to see swallowed whole
into the next, biggest, blackest
black hole in the universe.
His little hands and all.

I am taller, older than that Marla.
Every shade of melanin.
Every nail across a chalkboard
knows that's not my name!
Not Marlene. Marlena. Mariana.
Not Mar-Lana!
Marla, not even my nickname!

Please Don't Call Me "Ma'am"
My Black has not seriously cracked.
Yet you think I'm Methuselah, the Female?
I understand, your Momma
taught you to say "Thank You",
"Yes, please," and "Yes, Ma'am."
Crossing i's and dotting t's.
Uncrossing knees means less than you think
to Boomer women still working like me.

Please Don't Call Me "Miss"
cause I was married.
Every woman my age has
heard that single name.
We prayed not to hear it again.
Does any lash or limb on me
resemble Miss Daisy?

Please Don't Call Me "Ms."
Gloria Steinem, some of us prefer Mrs.
Only married long enough
to sign the marriage certificate.
Barely made our bed before he was dead.
Do not pity me. Do not pity me.

Please Don't Call Me "Girl"
like one of your great-great-great-great-great
great-great grandDaddy's house servants.
If you ever do, I will have to secretly
spit in your water glass or bowl of soup.
Too polite to spit on you.

Please Don't Call Me "Hun"
like I'm your dessert.
No, do not start.
The next word outta your mouth
better not be Honey, Sweetie, Sweetheart,
Sugar Plum or Sugar! No way, Baby!
I would never get inside your ice cream saucer.
Never lick spoons with you
when I barely know you.

Please Don't Ever Never Ever
Call Me the N-Word,
the B-Word, Angry, Sapphire,
Stupid, Low IQ, Very Dumb.
Crazy, Wacky. Deranged.
Neurotic! Horseface!
Off the Wall! OK boomer!
Not any Abominable Names!
I went to college ready to make my own bed.
Not afraid to sleep in it by myself.
Ready to reclaim our true names
we inherited long, long, long ago.

Please Call Me Queen.
Your Majesty. Your Highness.
Your Regalness.
Marlana. Marlana-Patrice.
Auntie. Aunt Marti.
Mrs. Hamer. Sister.
Gorgeous. Beautiful.
Reader. Speaker. Teacher.
Poet. Poetess.
I will answer.

Even Call Me "Mama"
Not the I-have-kids Mama
cause I have none.
Don't you ever pretend to be one.
Mama like you want me.
Like that flirty young man on the plane.
When he called me, Mama,
he put blush on my cheeks,
made me love my thick waist,
stop quarreling with my extra 50 pounds.
Made me forget about clicking my heels becoming 21 again.
Just —
    Please Don't Call Me "Marla."

Ode to My Glorious Two Feet

Remember our shoe catastrophes?
That epic time you caught me after
I somersaulted down that
slippery church stairwell?

You hesitated for an instant,
being flat since birth.
Erect again.
Feeling *Black Woman Natural*.
High in black heels.
At least four inches taller.

After EMS, determined to
wear my accident in style,
you begged and begged me
to elevate you. But NEVER,

NEVER like that again!
I agreed recalling
other shoe calamities.
Knowing none of those
were ever your fault.

No fun being upended by gravity.
Terrifying the hell out of me!
Not wanting to kiss concrete,
tile, or carpets ever again!

Not wanting to fall again.
For *Lust*, *Vanity*. *Other Human Frailties*.
Or be a churchgoer dressing for selfies,
not our true *Saviors*.

Not in the mood to admire my skies like that.
Ceilings or new designer shoes like that. Not unless we are both
standing together, looking forward, feeling upright and protected.
We are Walking. Walking. Walking to God's rhythm.

 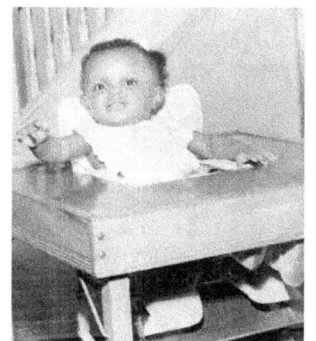 

ACKNOWLEDGMENTS

First and foremost, I must effusively thank my beloved late parents, Wiley Anthony and Louvenia Elizabeth Gillispie Pugh, who were there from the day I took my first breath to witnessing many creative milestones in my life. From reciting a poem in church to winning a poetry or speaking contest, they always loved and supported me, encouraged me to display all of my talents. "Never hide anything under a rock," they would say. They are both gone now, but I know they are smiling now, realizing that I finally wrote my first poetry book!

Several others along the way have been there for me — including my three siblings. A special salute to my baby brother, Wiley, who was there when I won second place in the Hessler Street Fair Poetry Contest in 2008 — you could say he became a fan then.

Special thanks to my Dad's older sister, Aunt C.B. She taught us how important it is to keep the epistolary tradition going, writing letters and keeping in touch with family. Our oldest relative to date, she passed at the age of 105.

There are so many other Cleveland poets and supporters worth mentioning including Dianne Borsenik, Jen Pezzo, Theresa Gottl Brightman, Ken Kitt, John Burroughs (United States Beat Poet Laureate, 2022-2023), Geri Burroughs, Steve Goldberg, Christina M. Brooks, Tim Herron, Milenko Budimir, Clarissa Jakobsons, Claire McMahon, Michael Salinger, and Hassan Rogers. Abundant thanks to Ray McNiece (Poet Laureate of Cleveland Heights, Ohio, 2020-2023). A Cleveland poetry legend, Ray gave me my first feature before I relocated to Arizona. Thanks also to The Poet's Haven and its legendary leader, VertigoXX (Vertigo Xi An Xavier) who gave me additional performance and publishing opportunities while I was still living in Cleveland. The Cleveland poetry community will always miss him. Gone too soon. Kudos to Dr. Mary Weems and Michael Oatman for publishing one of my poems in the amazing tribute anthology they edited. Thanks, Lois Collier, Naomi Gibbs, and Doris Meeks, my fellow teachers and friends, for being so encouraging before and after I relocated. Also, Edwina Young who has been a supportive friend since elementary school.

Praise to the accomplished English professors and poetry workshop instructors who inspired me while I lived in Cleveland. They include Nikki Giovanni, Dr. Audrey Thomas McCluskey, Dr. James Magner, Professor Joseph T. Cotter, Professor James C. Kilgore, Russell Atkins, Toi Derricotte, and David Mura. They all helped shape my poetic voice.

Praise to my Cleveland places and spaces that also made me become the poet I am today. Hoban Dominican where I first read *Hamlet*. Also *Romeo and Juliet*. John Carroll University, where I heard Gwendolyn Brooks speak about "Poetry is life distilled." My home church, St. James AME, where I recited Easter rhymes as a child and then, as an adult, performed poems by Maya Angelou and Gwendolyn Brooks during programs. Thank you to Karamu House, where I took poetry classes with Mr. Atkins, one of the first expirmental poets in this country, Cuyahoga Community College, where I attended writing workshops organized by Professor Kilgore. My Cleveland classrooms where I taught poetry and helped students write poetry books for Young Authors. Also thank you, Hessler Street Fair, Cleveland Slice, Poets in the Park, the Literary Cafe, Severance Hall, Cain Park, and the Cleveland Museum of Art. The Harvard-Lee and Shaker Heights Libraries, as well as the Main Cleveland Public Library. A Cultural Exchange, Mac's Backs, Waldenbooks, and Barnes & Noble.

While still living in Cleveland, I had the honor and pleasure of meeting three accomplished Ohio writers, Virginia Hamilton, Sharon Draper, and Jacqueline Woodson, all of whom inspired me to hone my craft as a storyteller.

Praise to traveled places where I learned to see the world more broadly and vividly, especially in regard to being a part of the Black Diaspora. Fortunately, I visited my parents' hometowns of Tuskegee, Alabama and Meridian, Mississippi before they died. Both parents took the Alabama trip with sister Michelle and me. We also took historic trips together to Washington D.C., Atlanta, and Ontario. As a Lead Teacher with the Great Migration Project, I took three glorious summer trips to Charleston, South Carolina. Thank you, Ohio visionaries, Dr. Peter Rutkoff and Dr. Will Scott of Kenyon College for being at the Great Migration Project's helm. Thanks also to Dr. Mark Tebeau.

My Arizona thanks must go to fellow creatives and supporters: Rory Steele, Cathy Delaleu, Joanne Joshua, Marcy Poletick, Marguerite Tolliver, Serena "Wisdom Soul" Richardson, Cassandra Hall, Chanel Bragg, Patrice "MysticBlu" Stewart, Vaughn Willis, Suzy Jacobson Cherry, Rod Ambrose, Dr. Tamika Sanders, Jason Lalli, Jake Friedman, Andy Rodriguez, Ramona Ferrara, Carnell Thurman, Penny Phelan, Karen Bennett, Juniper Dery-Chaffin, MaryEllen Aschauer, and Spencer Howard. A special shoutout to two BlackPoet Ventures visionaries, Poets Leah Marche and Robert "Flipside" Daniels, who both encouraged me to perform at HomeBase. Thank you, other Arizona visionaries, Poet Harold Branch III, the founder of HomeBase, as well as Professor Gershom Williams, and Ms. Clottee Hammons, the Creative Director of Emancipation Arts. And thank you, Floyd Alvin Galloway, former Arizona Informant photojournalist and host of The Alvin Galloway Show.

Abundant thanks to another visionary, Dr. Neal A. Lester, Professor of English and Founding Director of Project Humanities at Arizona State University. He encouraged me, especially during the COVID-19 global pandemic, to keep writing, performing, and publishing. In fact, he was my literary godfather, the one who sent me the link to apply for the Community Literature Initiative Publishing Program, where I finally completed this book.

Thanks to Arizona places and spaces. The Virginia Piper Center for Creative Writing, where I attended my first Arizona State University poetry workshop. I wrote my first draft of "Dribble" there. Much gratitude to the ASU Desert Nights, Rising Stars Writers Conference 2021 where I gained so much new knowledge about poetry and writing. Mahogany L. Browne and Lyzette Wanzer were two of the dynamic facilitators. Poet and novelist Linda Hogan was the powerful keynote speaker. Thank you to many other organizations that host outstanding online poetry workshops and other literary events, including Poets & Writers. Performing at various online open mics continues to help me become a better poet.

Next, endless thanks to my special CLIque: Our CLI visionary and captain, Hiram Sims, who inspires so many. Many thanks to Andrés Sánchez, Anne Marie Wells, Marissa Forbes, James Coats, Estela Victoria-Cordero, Angela Cluley (AC), and Ashanti Webster, who all helped me immensely in the final stages of my manuscript. And to the rest of my CLI classmates in both Seasons 9 and 10, my alumni classmates, our guest poets, and all other CLI staff — I couldn't have finished this book without all of you! In addition, thank you for the CLI Special Sessions; those are invaluable. Special thanks to Emily Anne Evans, Press Manager of World Stage Press. Also to Benin Lemus, DeMisty D. Bellinger, and Antoinette Vella Payne.

The highest honor and praise must go to God, who gave me my talents — and then taught me to keep listening for the words. And they come often, like miraculous rain from Heaven. God, all praise to you for making me one of your earthly vessels.

Much love and gratitude to all those who have helped me finally write this book — because its arrival is, without question, an auspicious one. I welcome it.

Before finding a home in this book, the following were previously published:
- "Possessions," *2008 Hessler Street Fair Poetry Anthology.*
- "This Is a Man's World," *Say It Loud!: Poems about James Brown.*
- "Flight Lessons," *1619 Speaks: An Anthology of African American Poetry*

ABOUT THE AUTHOR

Marlana-Patrice Pugh Hamer (she/her) is an award-winning poet, writer, performer, public speaker, educator, and volunteer/activist. She has been writing poetry since the age of nine, with a small spiral notebook—her "first poetry book"—as living proof. *Taking Off My Black & White Saddle Shoes: Cleveland Poems* is her first published collection of poetry.

Throughout the years, Marlana has been a contributing poet and writer to various anthologies, including a creative nonfiction piece published in *Indiscernibles in Arizona: On the Hope and Reality of Being Black in Arizona*. Her poetry has appeared in *1619 Speaks: An Anthology of African American Poets, Dimepiece: Ten Years of CLI Poetry, Sandcutters 2023,* and *Say It Loud!: Poems about James Brown*, among others.

Her awards include first place at the the District 10 Humorous Speech Contest, Toastmasters International, Inc. in 1994. In 2008, her poem, "Possessions, Part II" won second place in the Annual Hessler Street Fair Poetry Contest in Cleveland, Ohio. A native Clevelander, Marlana participated in multiple open mics before relocating to the Phoenix Metropolitan area in 2009, where she performs her poetry and features at special community events regularly.

She has a B.A. in English from John Carroll University and an M. Ed. in Curriculum and Instruction from Indiana Wesleyan University. Marlana is a veteran English and reading teacher who has taught on many levels, including teaching Freshman Composition at Purdue University. A lifelong learner, she has also completed several graduate-level courses beyond her two degrees. She is a proud alum of Community Literature Initiative (CLI), is a Teaching Assistant for the CLI Poetry Publishing Class, and continues to hone her craft by reading and writing daily, as well as attending poetry workshops—particularly ones focused on social justice.

A Project Humanities 101® Founder (ASU), she also volunteers for groups like Mission for Arizona and Save Our Schools Arizona. Since relocating, Marlana-Patrice has found more time to devote to other interests including photography, walking, hiking, yoga, cooking, decorating, and gardening. She also loves spending time with her friends and extended family members, including grandnieces and grandnephews.

Marlana's favorite time of the day is morning. She is always grateful to God for another sunrise.

linktr.ee/marlanapph
Instagram: @marlanapph